The Adventures of Strawberryhead & Gingerbread

The Barking Lot Series ④
Cursive Writing Workbook of the 50 US States!

The Adventures of Strawberryhead & Gingerbread

The Barking Lot Series ④
Cursive Writing Workbook of the 50 US States!

KF Wheatie & KM Wheatie

Strawberryhead &
Gingerbread Press

www.strawberryheadandgingerbread.com

The Adventures of Strawberryhead & Gingerbread,
The Barking Lot Series (4) Cursive Writing Workbook of the 50 US States!

Published by Strawberryhead and Gingerbread Press
https://www.strawberryheadandgingerbread.com

Copyright © 2024 by KF Wheatie & KM Wheatie

ISBN: 979-8-9894956-9-6

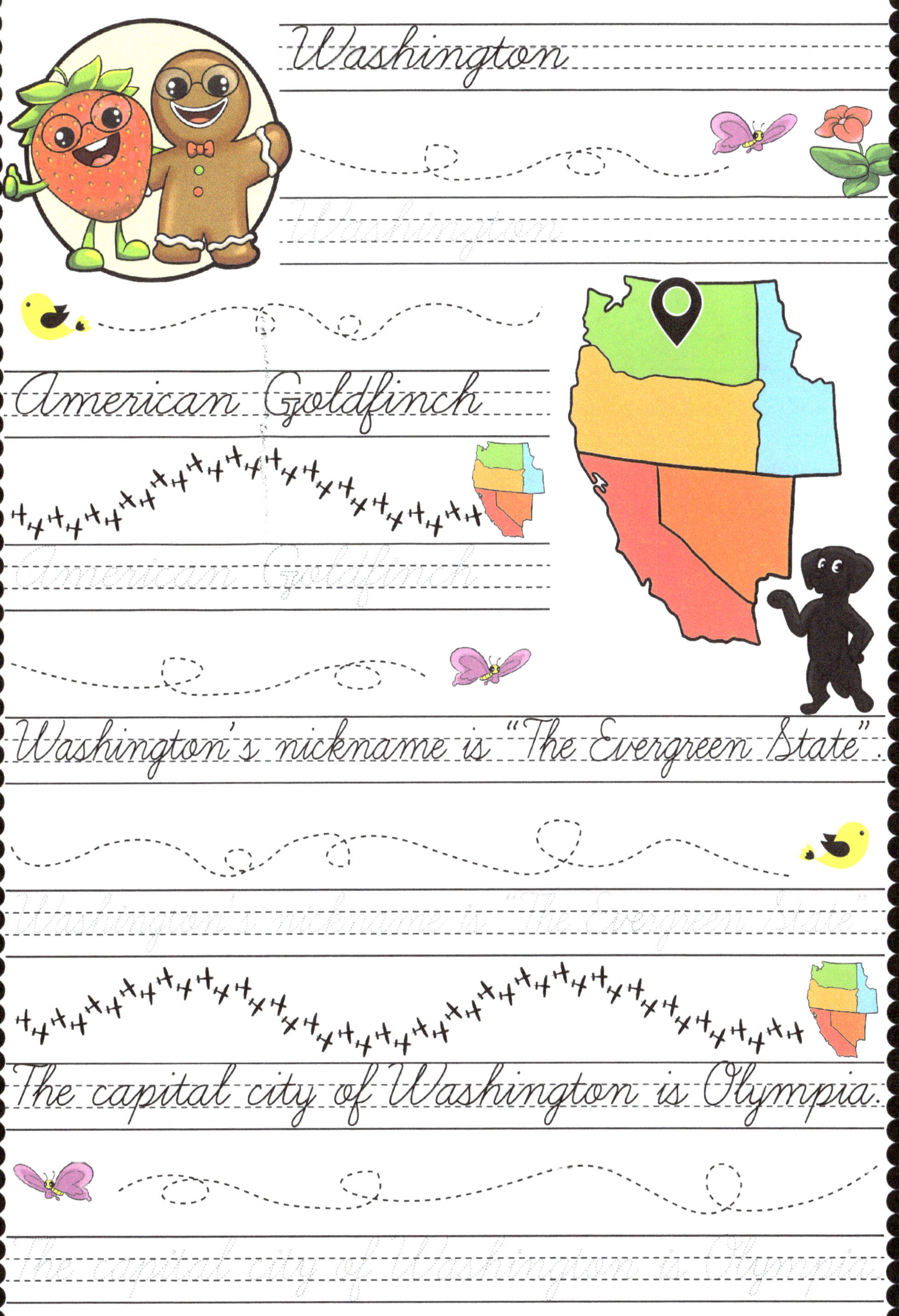

Washington

Washington

American Goldfinch

American Goldfinch

Washington's nickname is "The Evergreen State"

Washington's nickname is "The Evergreen State"

The capital city of Washington is Olympia.

The capital city of Washington is Olympia.

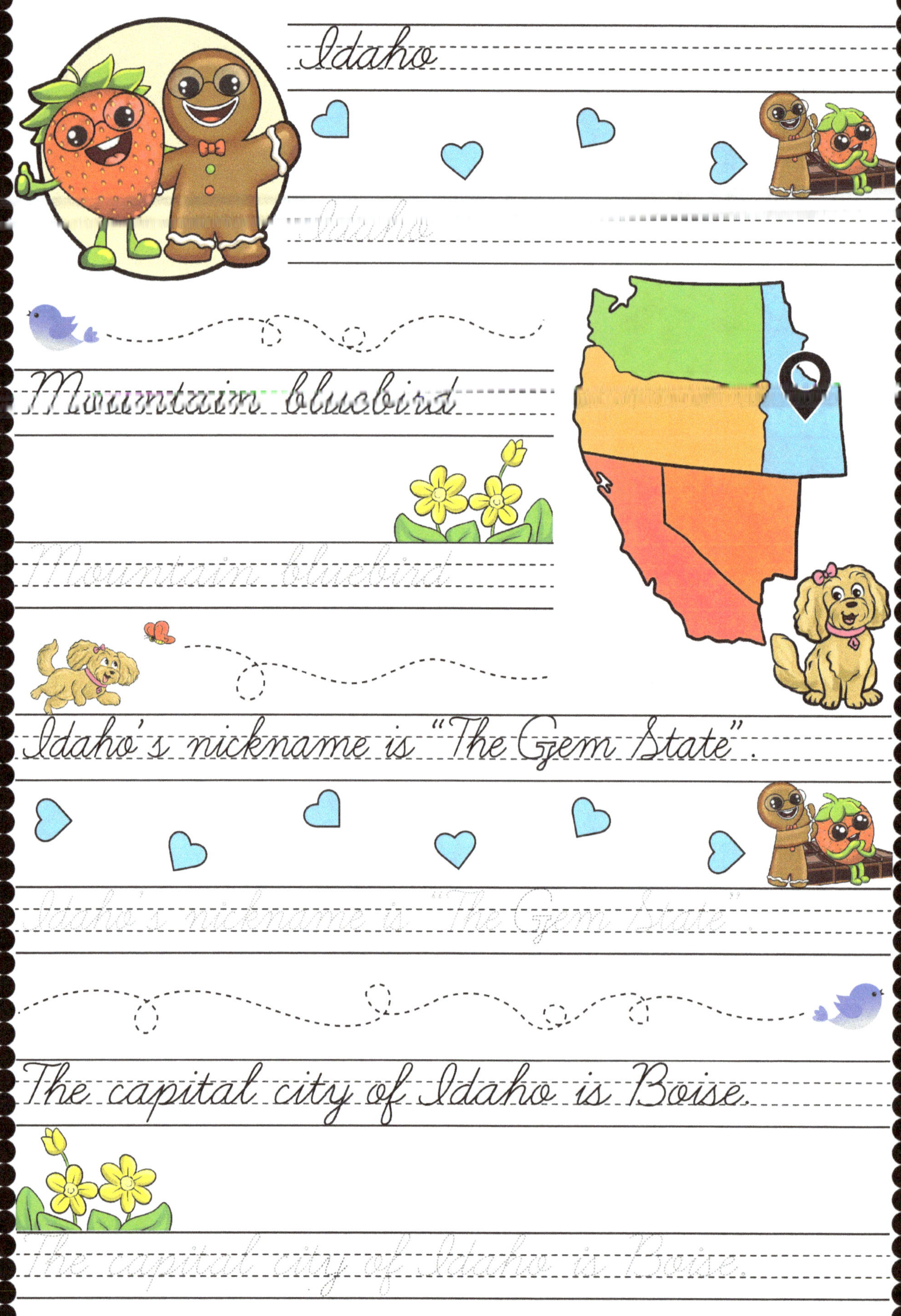

Idaho
Idaho
Mountain bluebird
Mountain bluebird
Idaho's nickname is "The Gem State".
Idaho's nickname is "The Gem State".
The capital city of Idaho is Boise.
The capital city of Idaho is Boise.

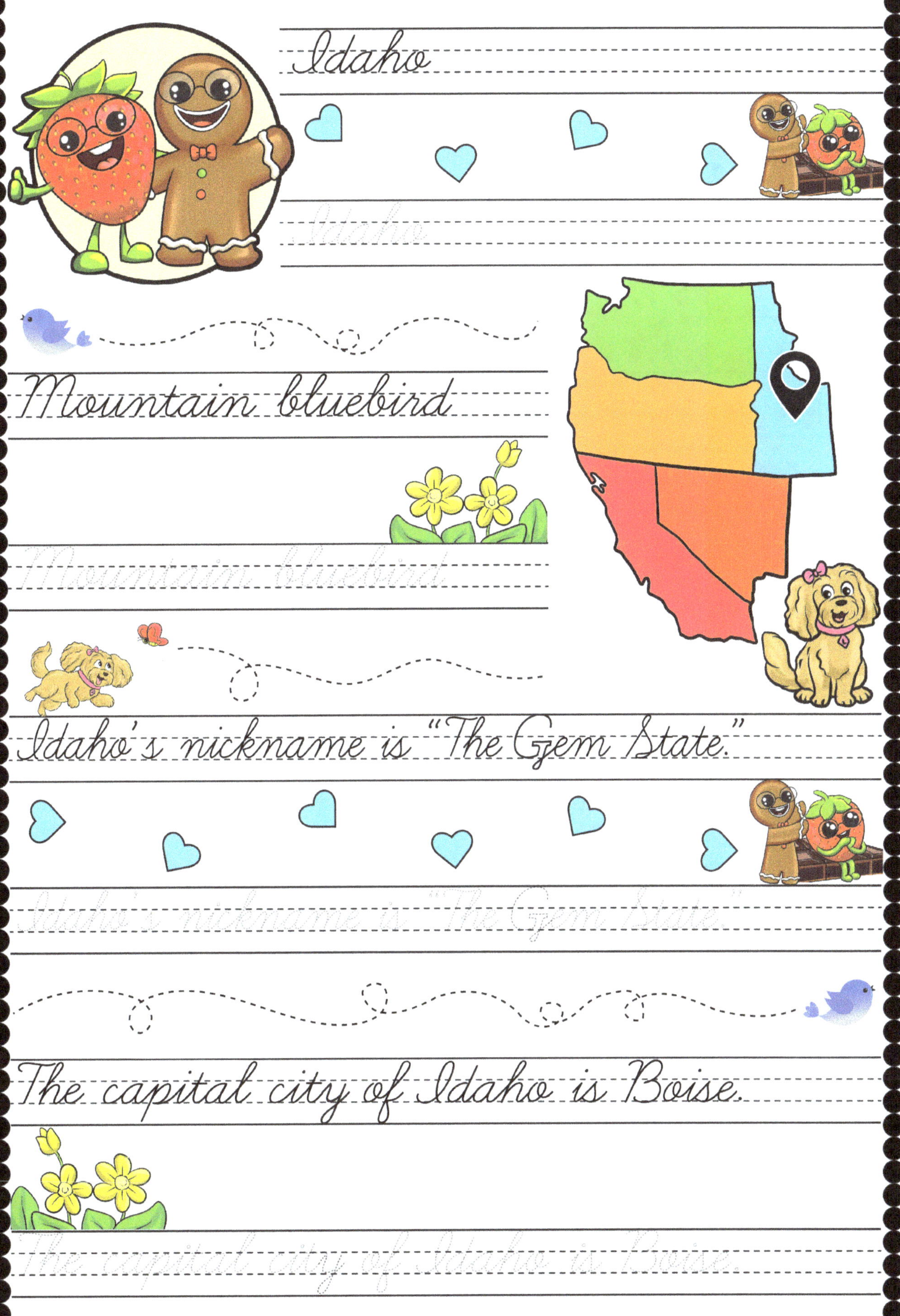

Idaho

Mountain bluebird

Idaho's nickname is "The Gem State."

The capital city of Idaho is Boise.

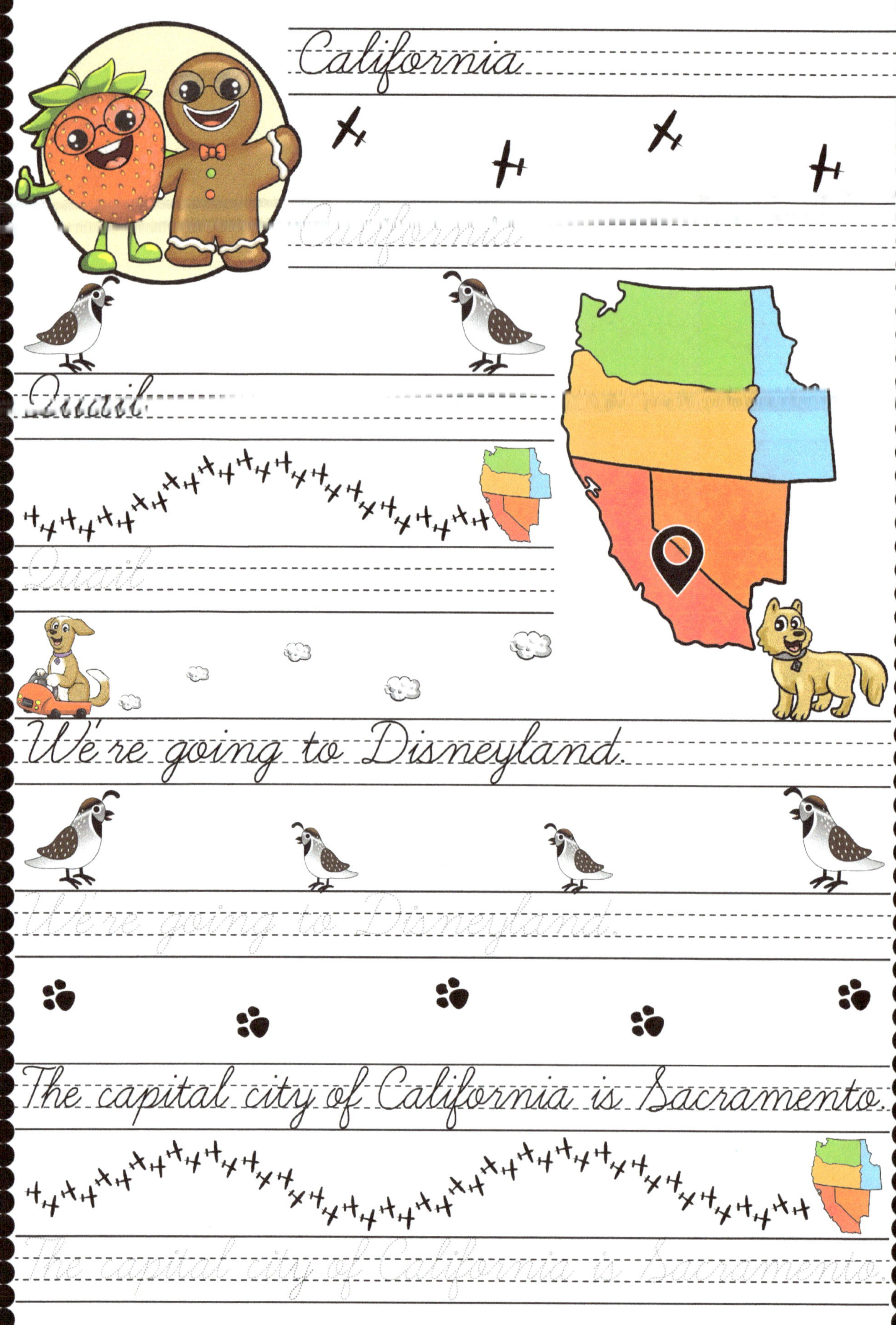

California

Quail

We're going to Disneyland.

The capital city of California is Sacramento.

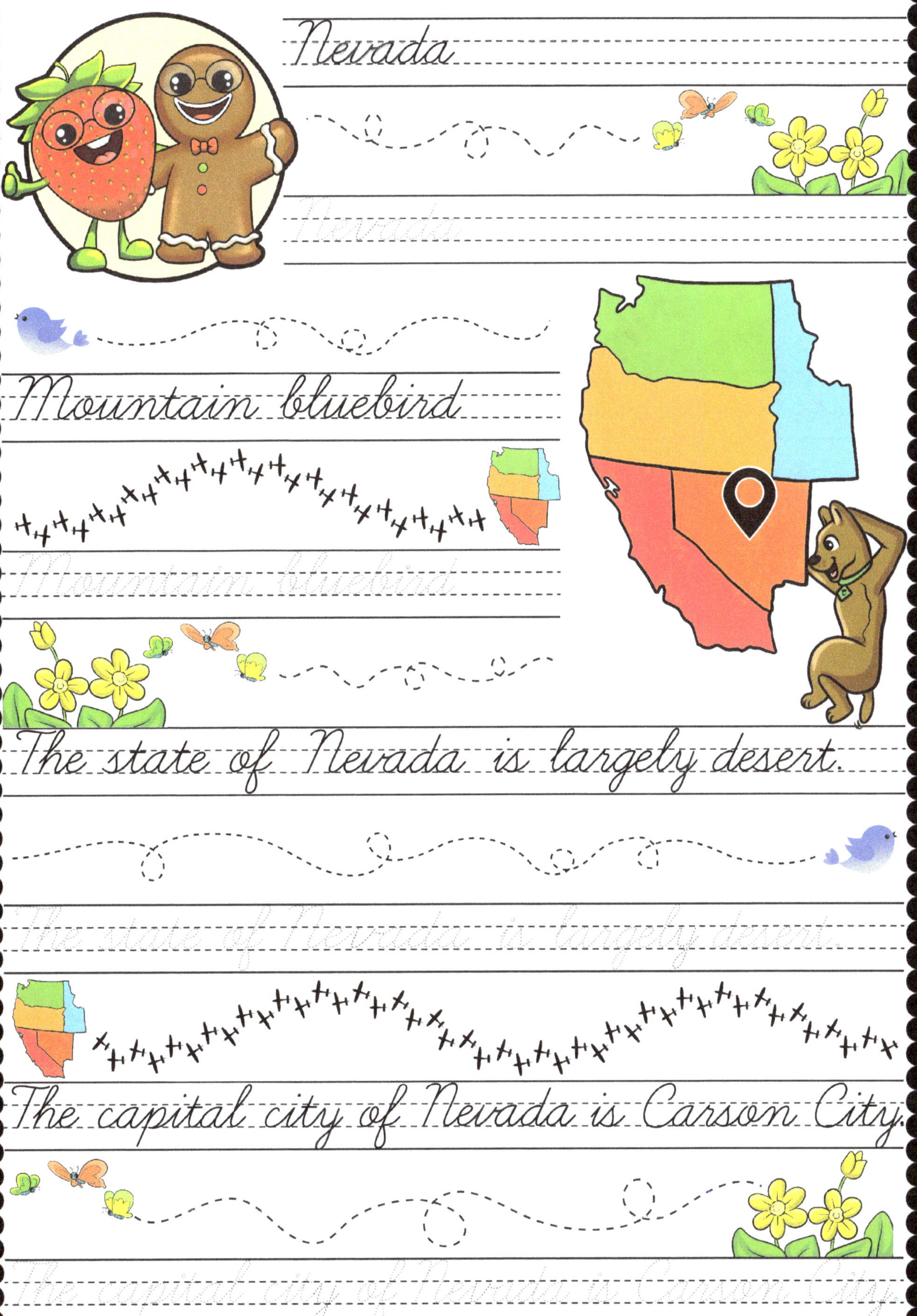

Nevada

Nevada

Mountain bluebird

Mountain bluebird

The state of Nevada is largely desert.

The state of Nevada is largely desert.

The capital city of Nevada is Carson City.

The capital city of Nevada is Carson City.

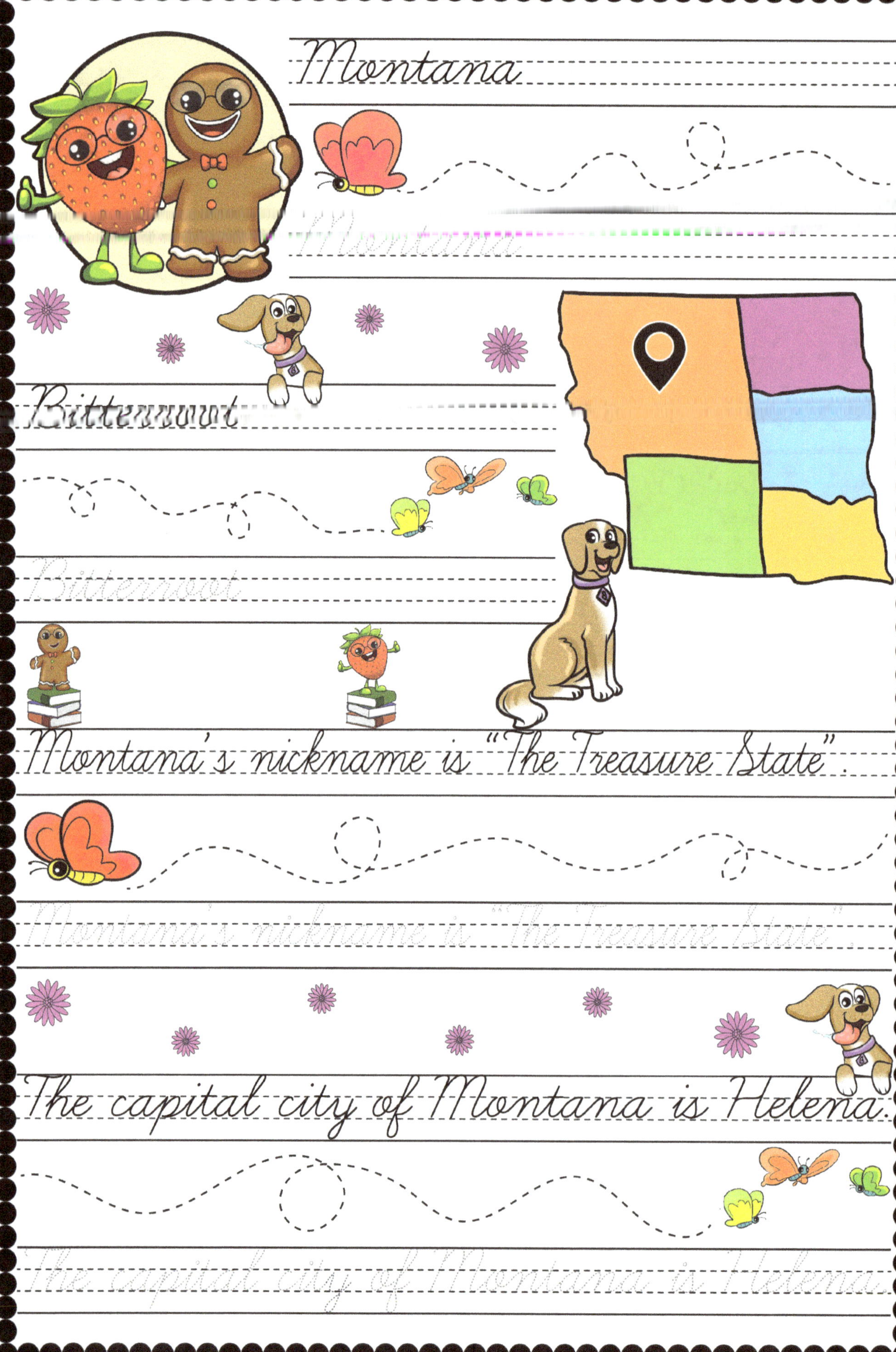

Montana

Montana

Bitterroot

Bitterroot

Montana's nickname is "The Treasure State".

Montana's nickname is "The Treasure State".

The capital city of Montana is Helena.

The capital city of Montana is Helena.

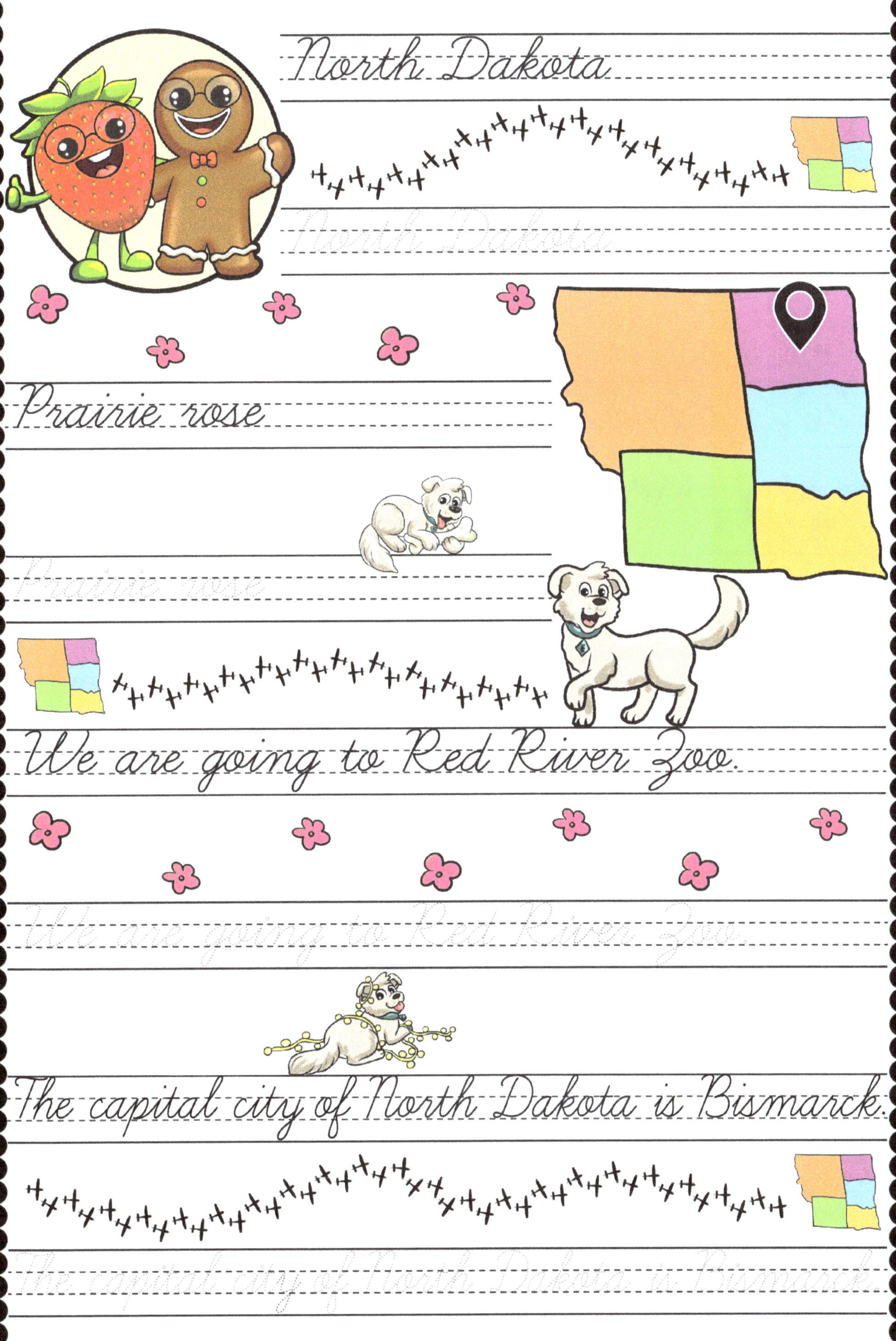

North Dakota

Prairie rose

We are going to Red River Zoo.

The capital city of North Dakota is Bismarck.

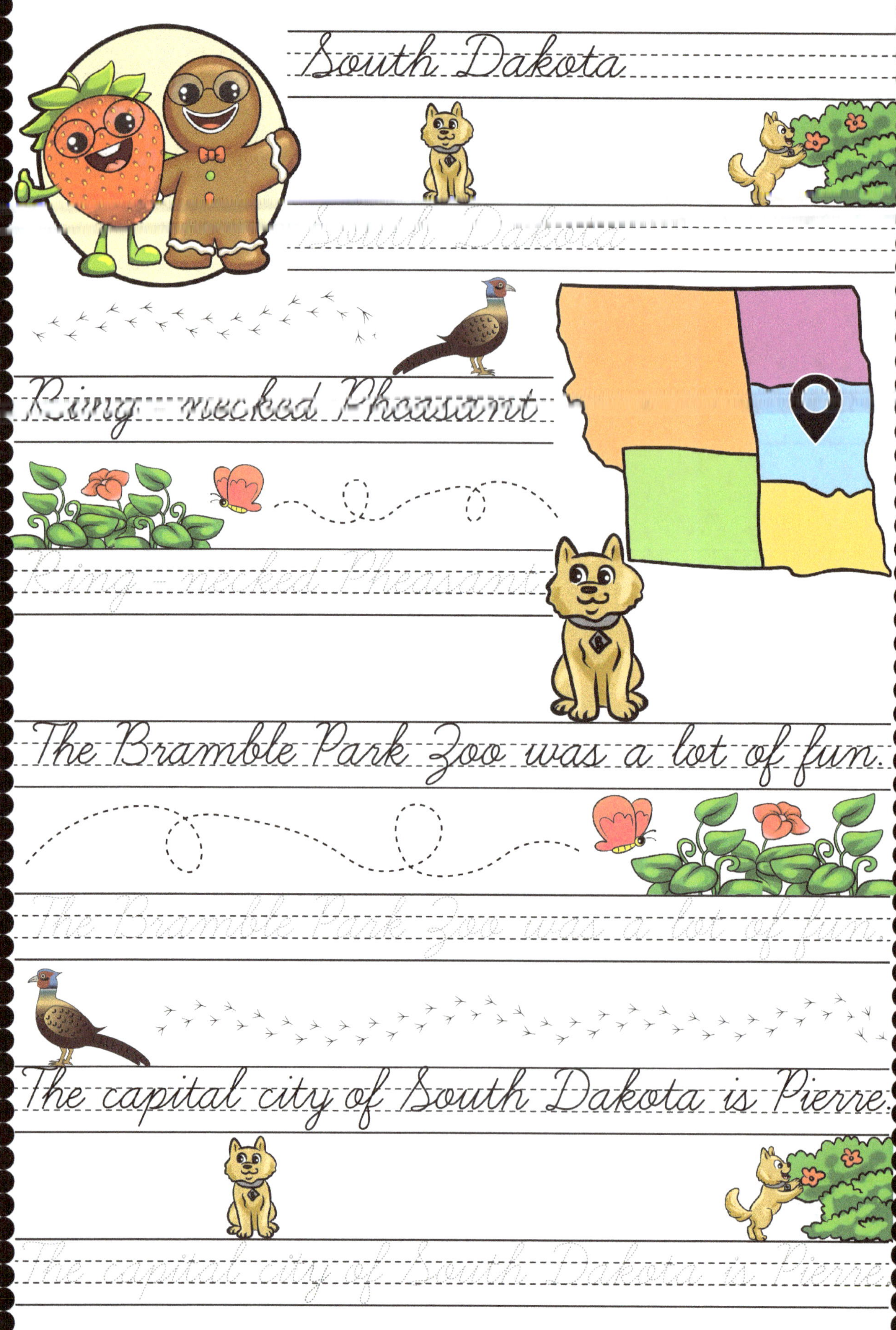

South Dakota

Ring-necked Pheasant

The Bramble Park Zoo was a lot of fun.

The capital city of South Dakota is Pierre.

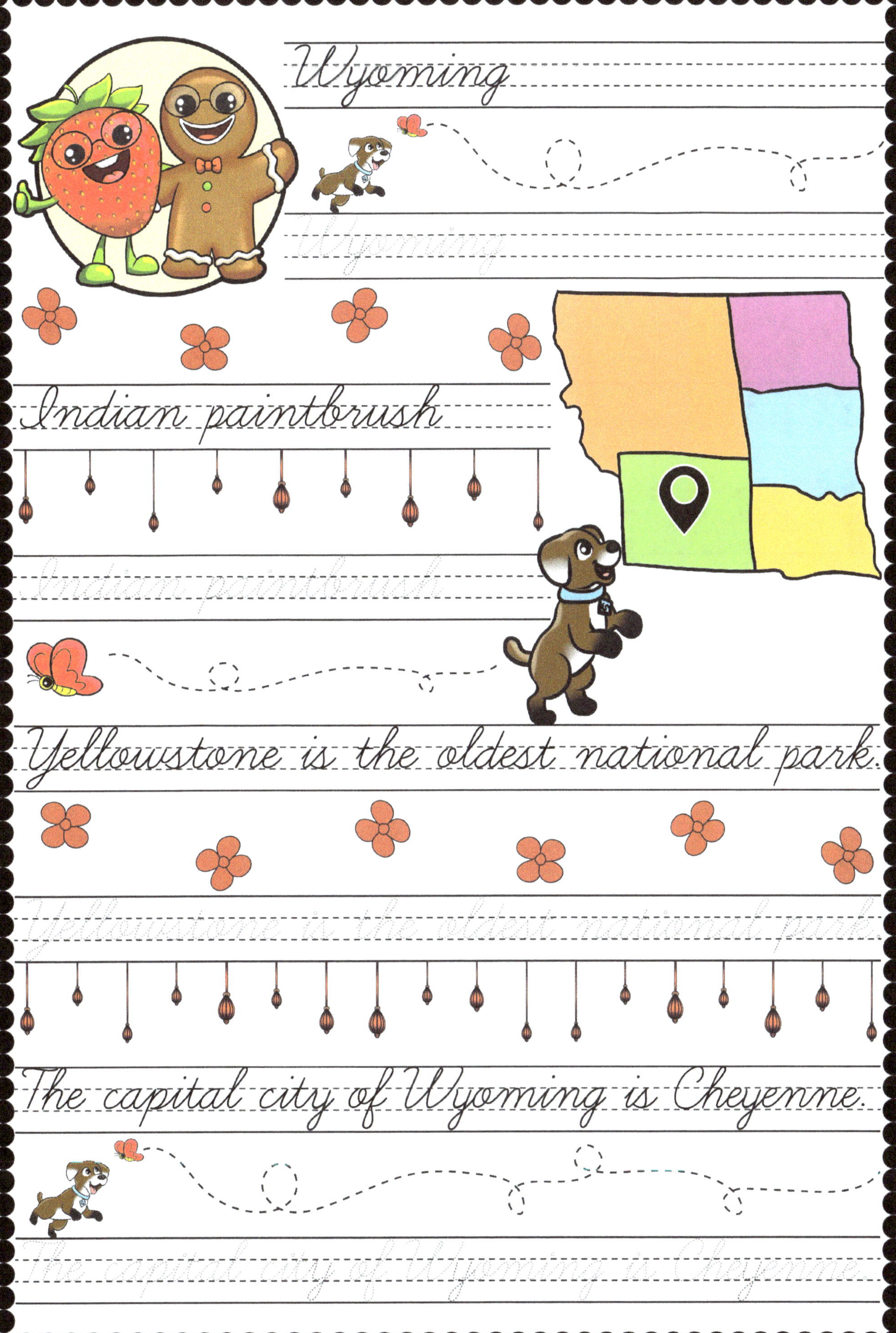

Wyoming

Wyoming

Indian paintbrush

Indian paintbrush

Yellowstone is the oldest national park.

Yellowstone is the oldest national park.

The capital city of Wyoming is Cheyenne.

The capital city of Wyoming is Cheyenne.

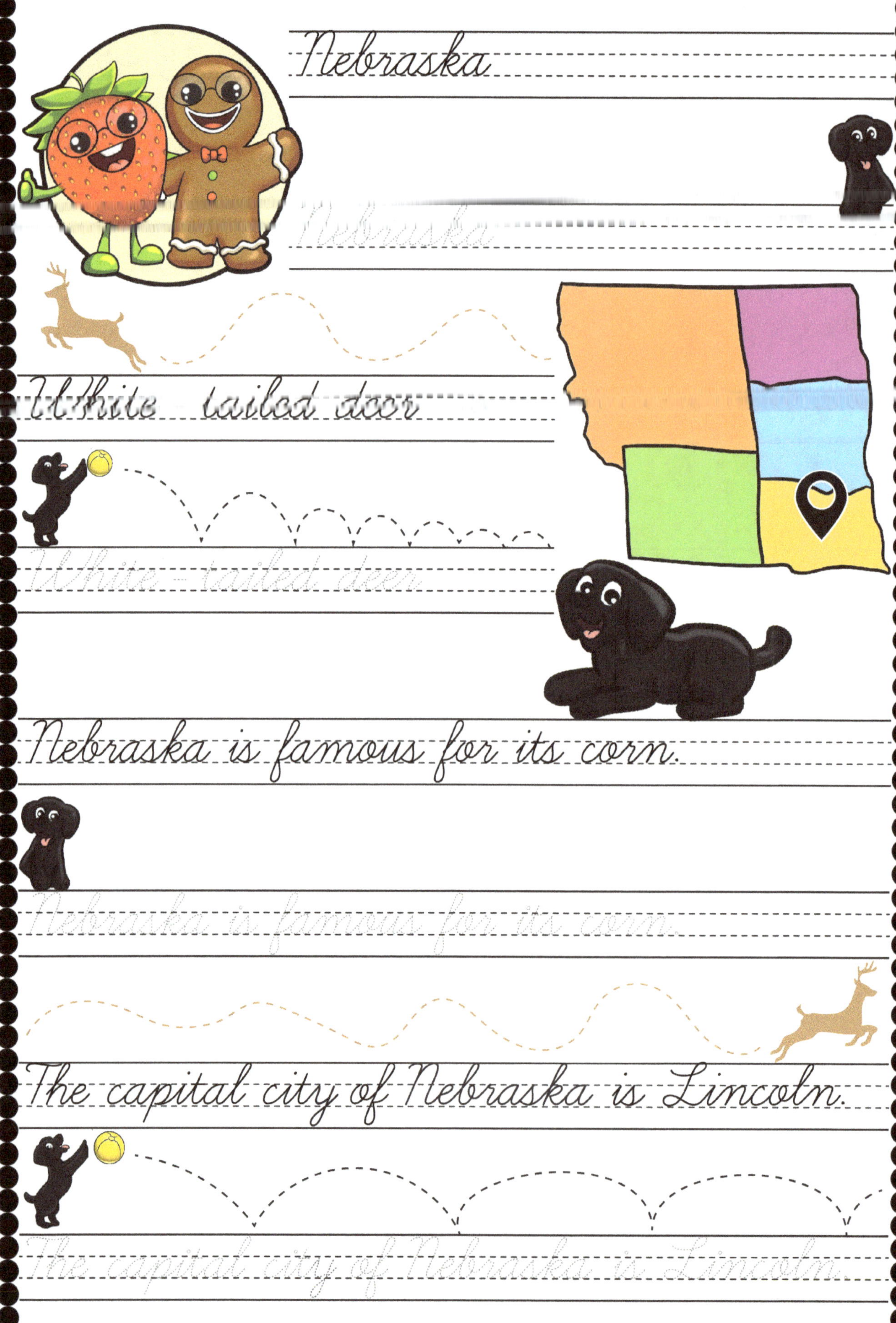

Nebraska

White_tailed deer

Nebraska is famous for its corn.

The capital city of Nebraska is Lincoln.

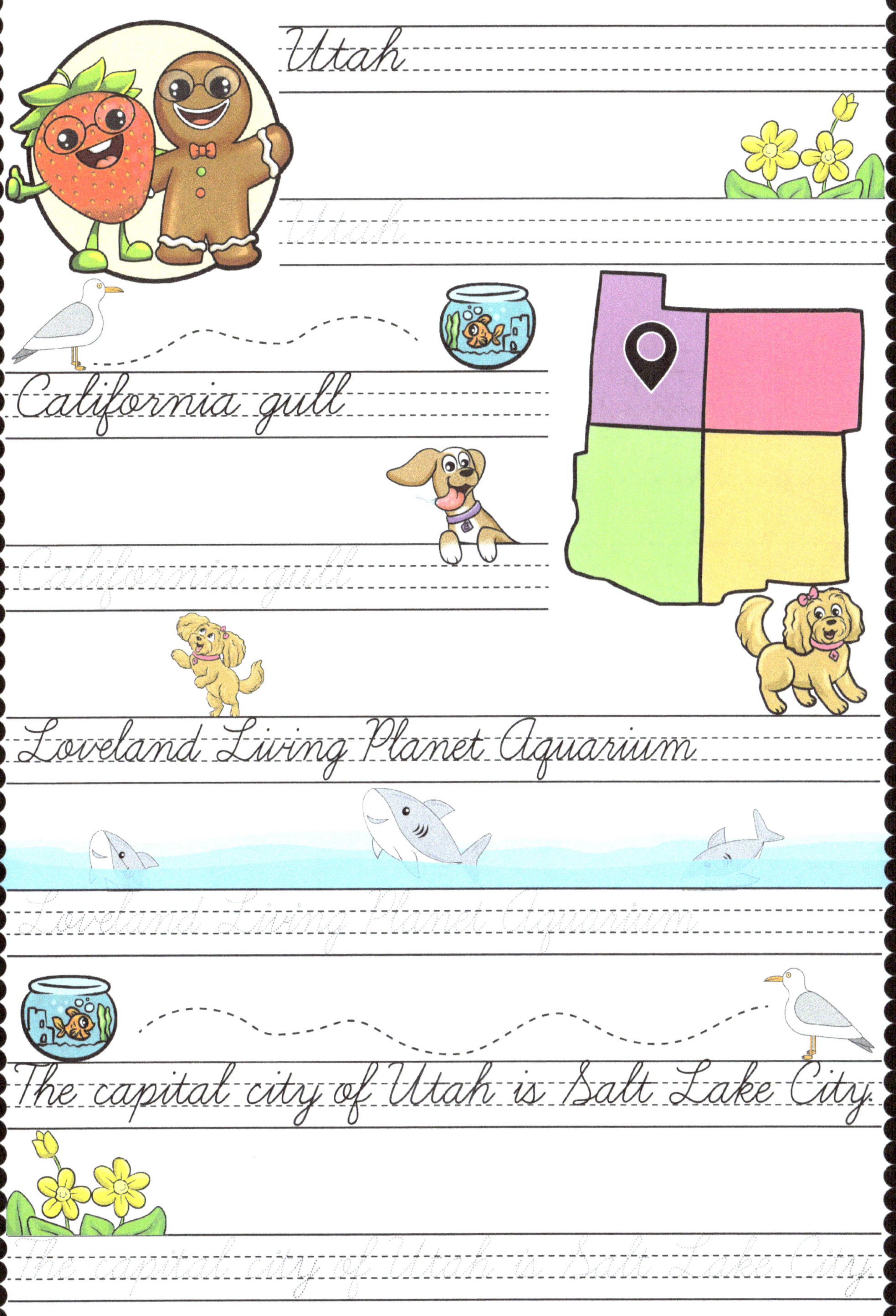

Utah

Utah

California gull

California gull

Loveland Living Planet Aquarium

Loveland Living Planet Aquarium

The capital city of Utah is Salt Lake City.

The capital city of Utah is Salt Lake City.

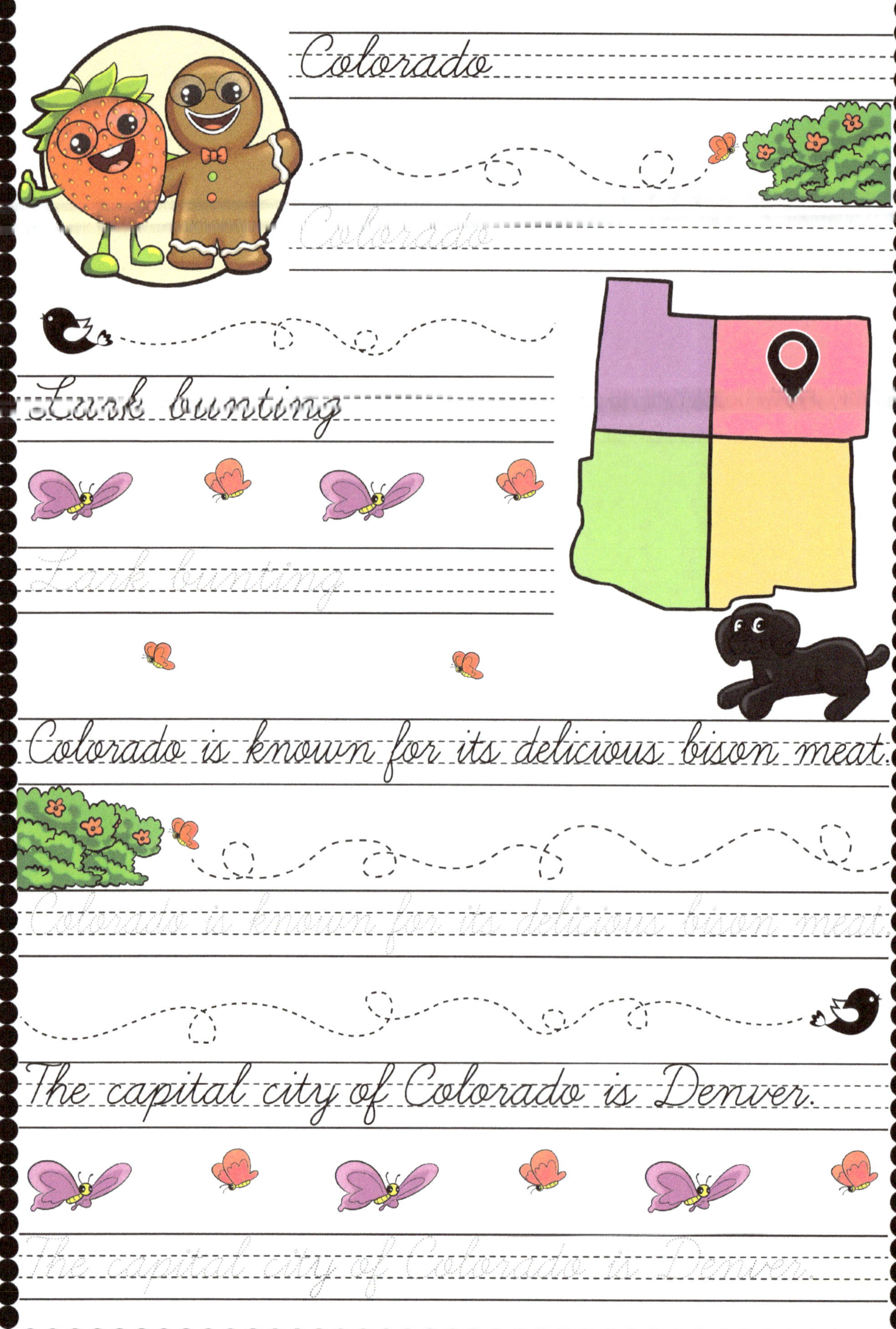

Colorado

Colorado

Lark bunting

Lark bunting

Colorado is known for its delicious bison meat.

Colorado is known for its delicious bison meat.

The capital city of Colorado is Denver.

The capital city of Colorado is Denver.

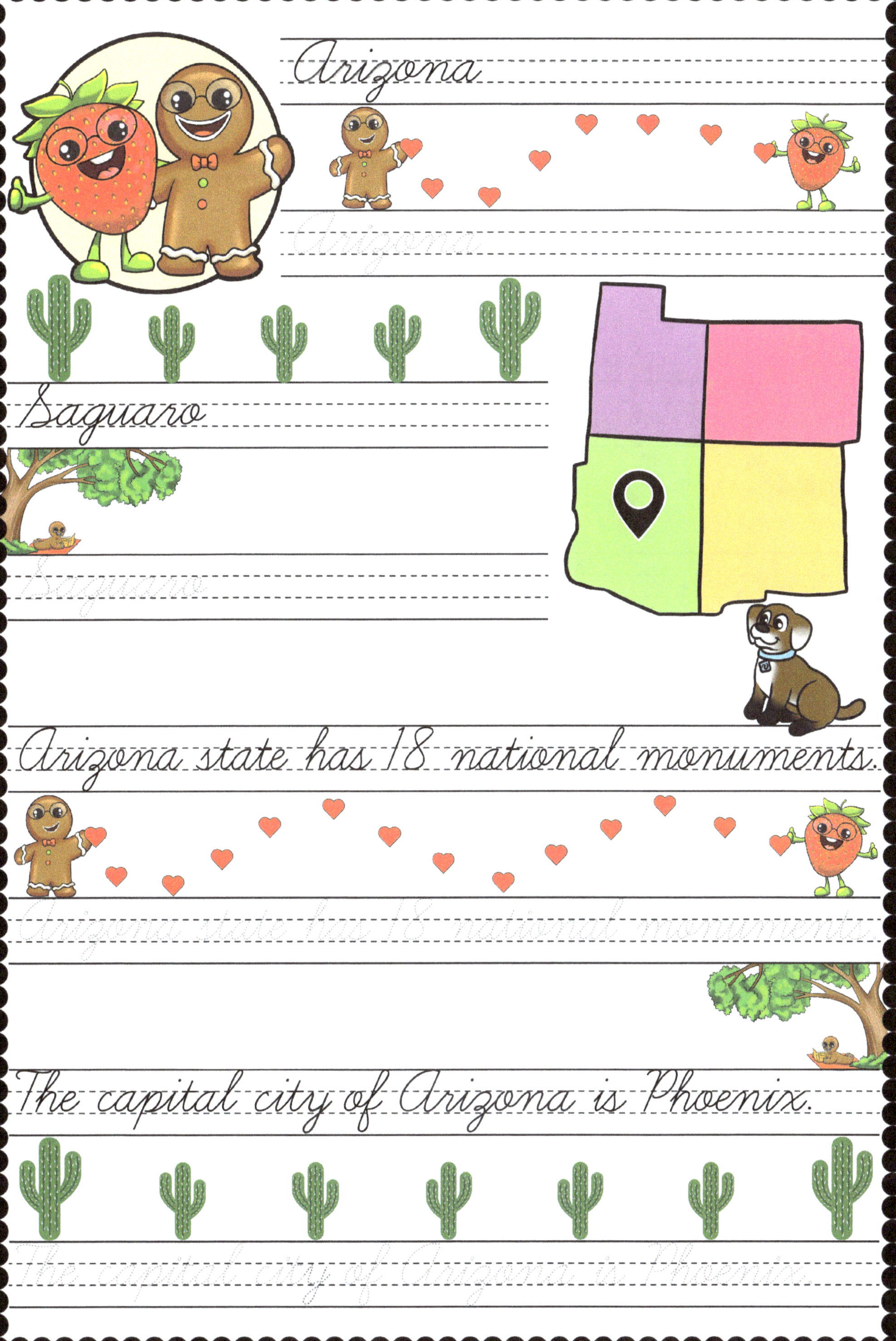

Arizona

Arizona

Saguaro

Saguaro

Arizona state has 18 national monuments.

Arizona state has 18 national monuments.

The capital city of Arizona is Phoenix.

The capital city of Arizona is Phoenix.

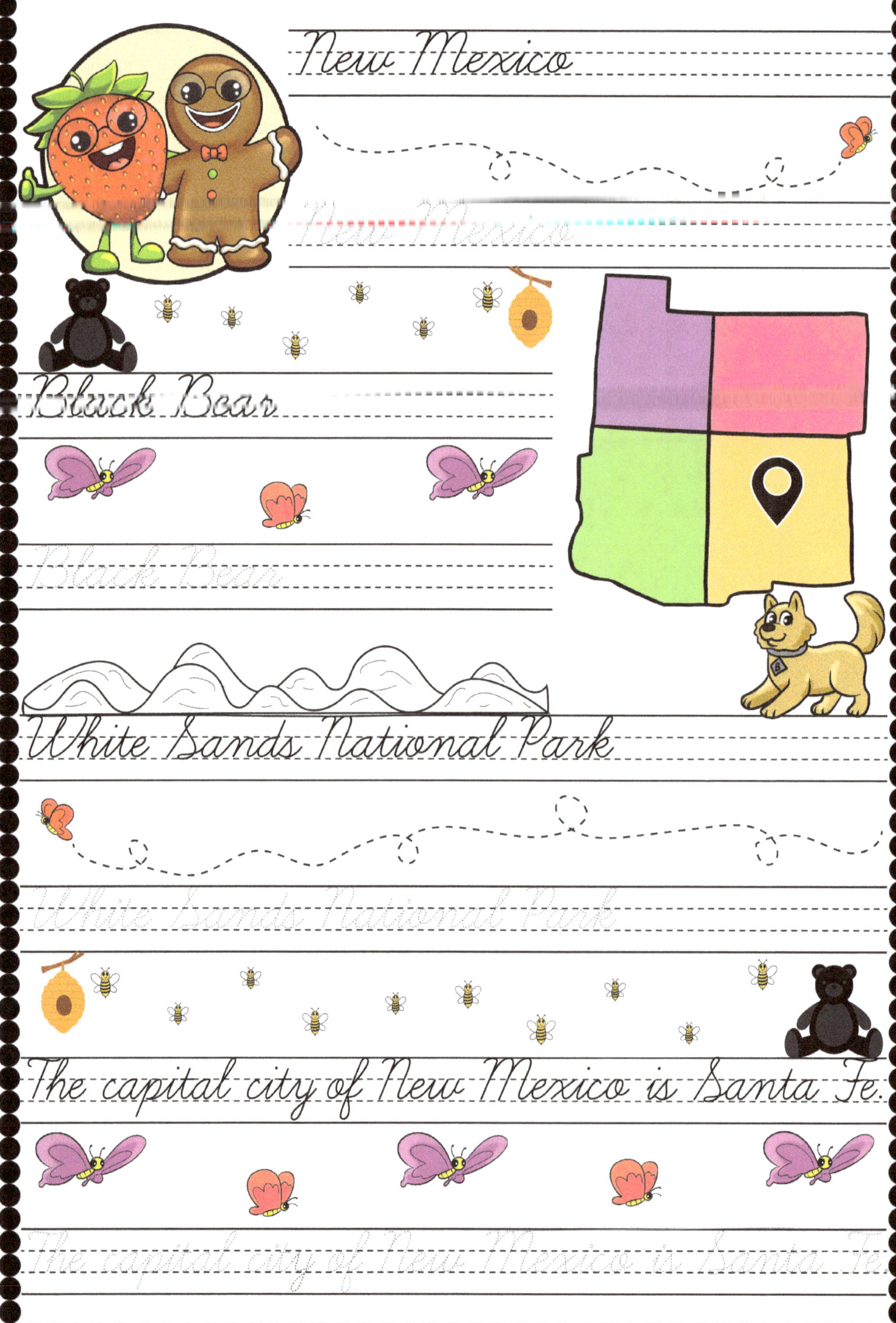

New Mexico

New Mexico

Black Bear

Black Bear

White Sands National Park

White Sands National Park

The capital city of New Mexico is Santa Fe.

The capital city of New Mexico is Santa Fe.

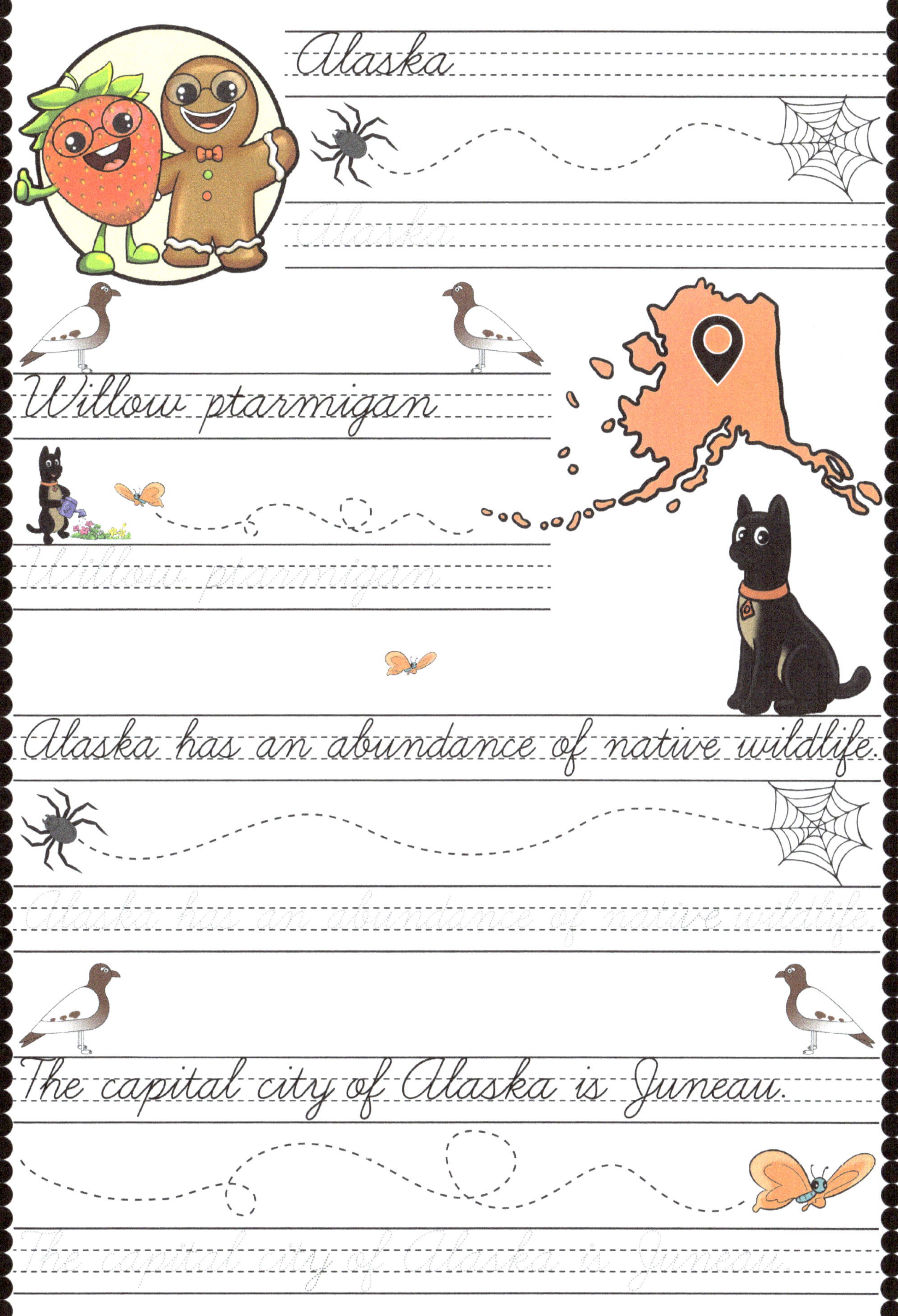

Alaska
Alaska
Willow ptarmigan
Willow ptarmigan
Alaska has an abundance of native wildlife.
Alaska has an abundance of native wildlife.
The capital city of Alaska is Juneau.
The capital city of Alaska is Juneau.

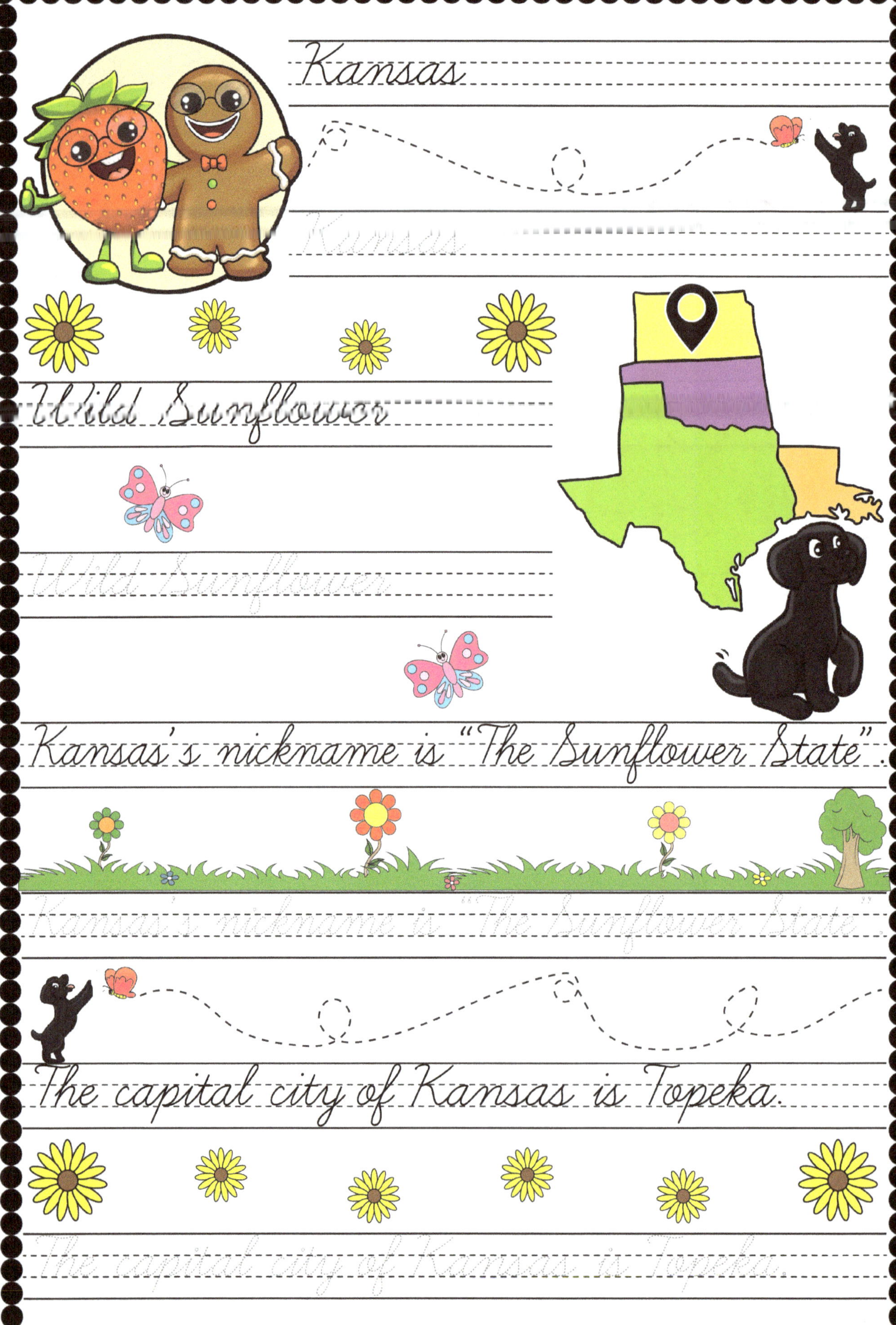

Kansas

Wild Sunflower

Kansas's nickname is "The Sunflower State".

The capital city of Kansas is Topeka.

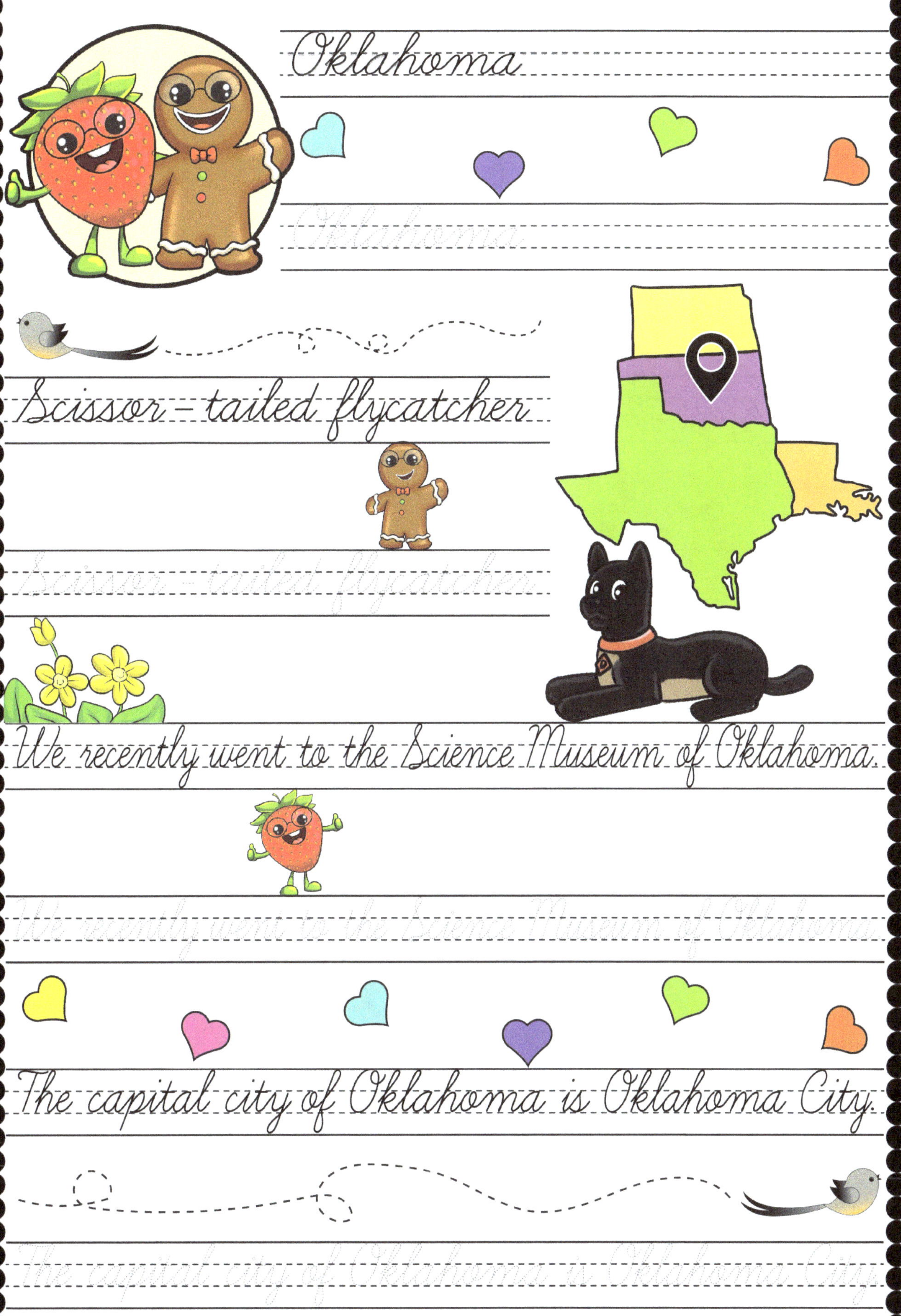

Oklahoma

Oklahoma

Scissor-tailed flycatcher

Scissor-tailed flycatcher

We recently went to the Science Museum of Oklahoma.

We recently went to the Science Museum of Oklahoma.

The capital city of Oklahoma is Oklahoma City.

The capital city of Oklahoma is Oklahoma City.

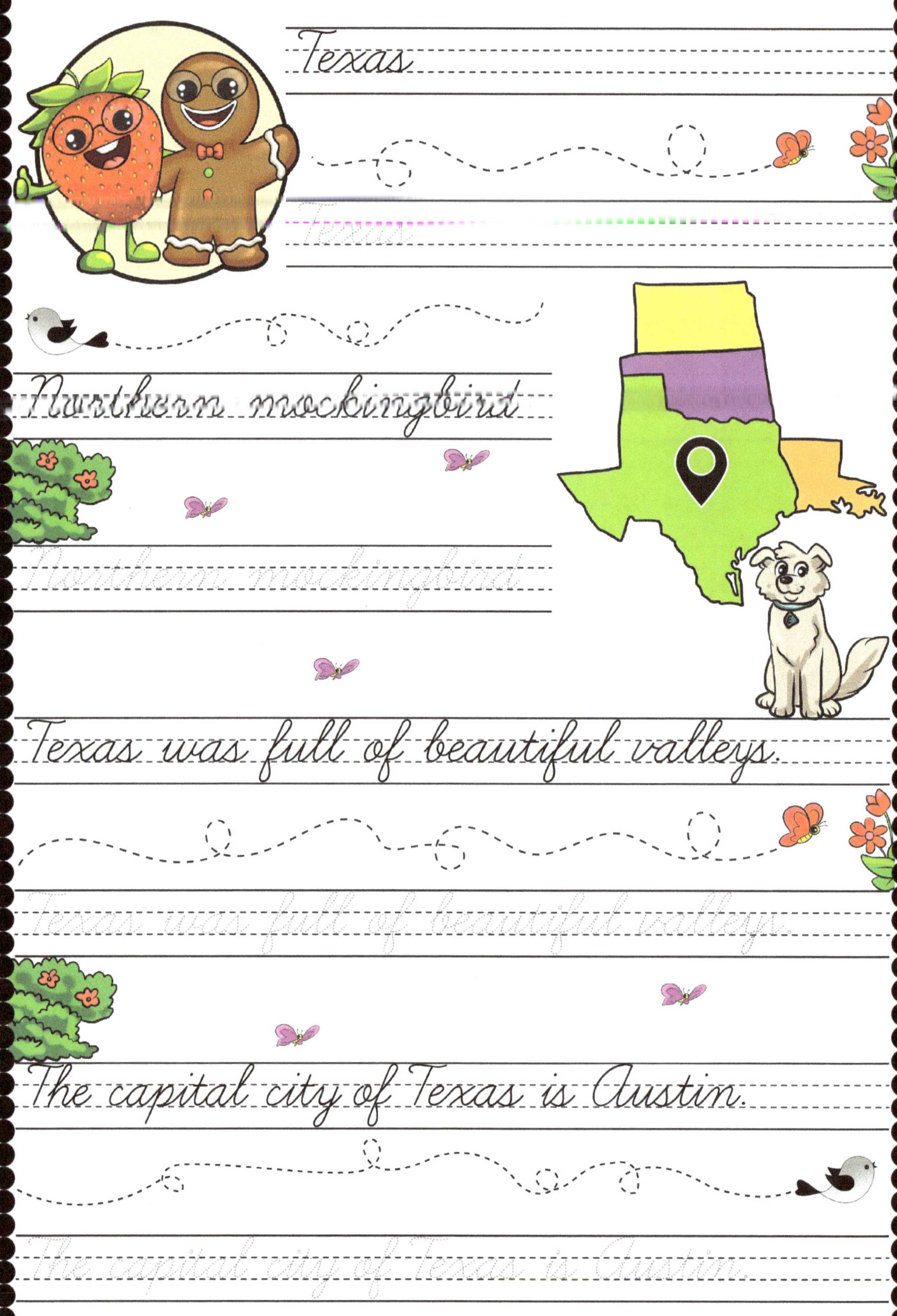

Texas

Texas

Northern mockingbird

Northern mockingbird

Texas was full of beautiful valleys.

Texas was full of beautiful valleys.

The capital city of Texas is Austin.

The capital city of Texas is Austin.

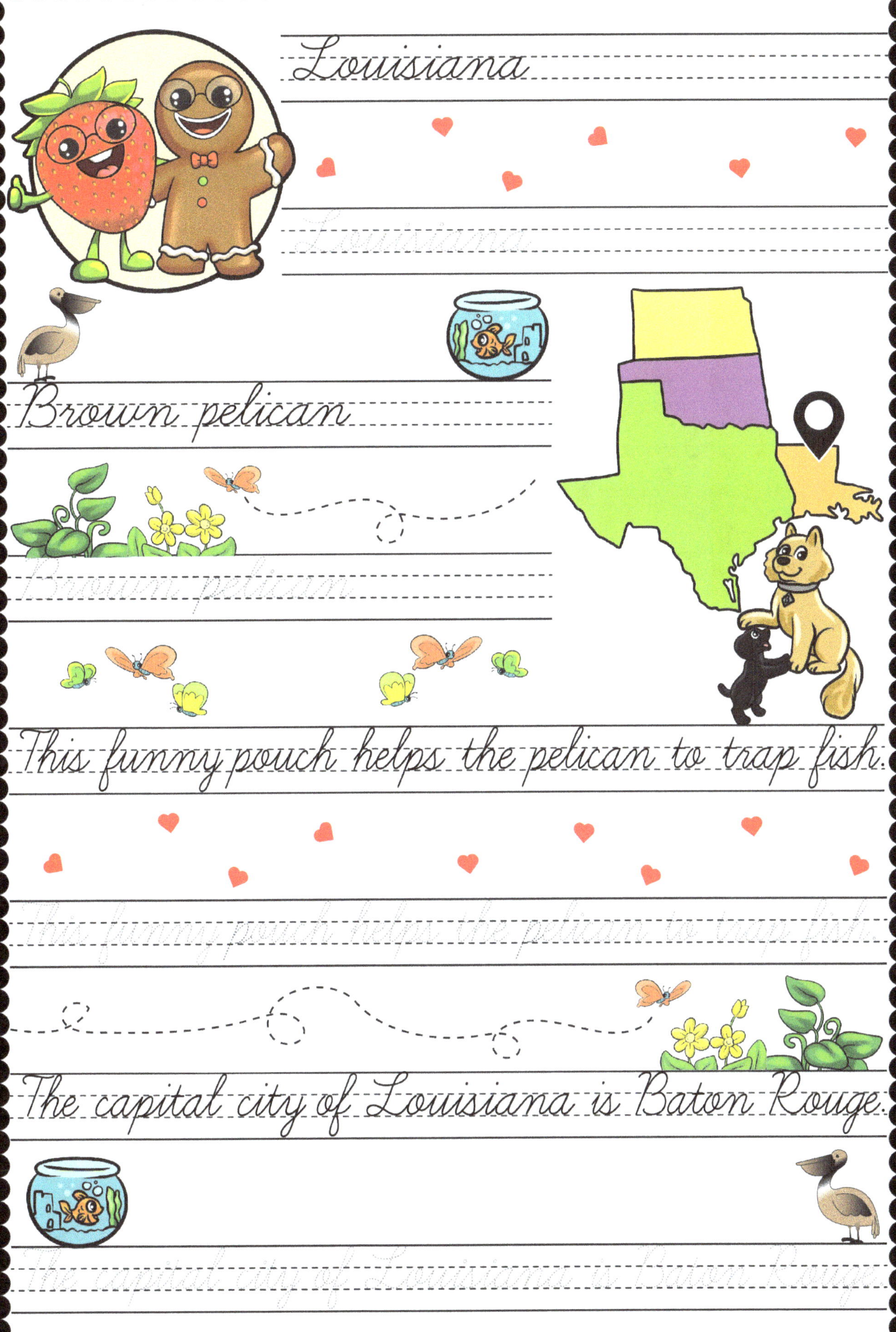

Louisiana

Louisiana

Brown pelican

Brown pelican

This funny pouch helps the pelican to trap fish.

This funny pouch helps the pelican to trap fish.

The capital city of Louisiana is Baton Rouge.

The capital city of Louisiana is Baton Rouge.

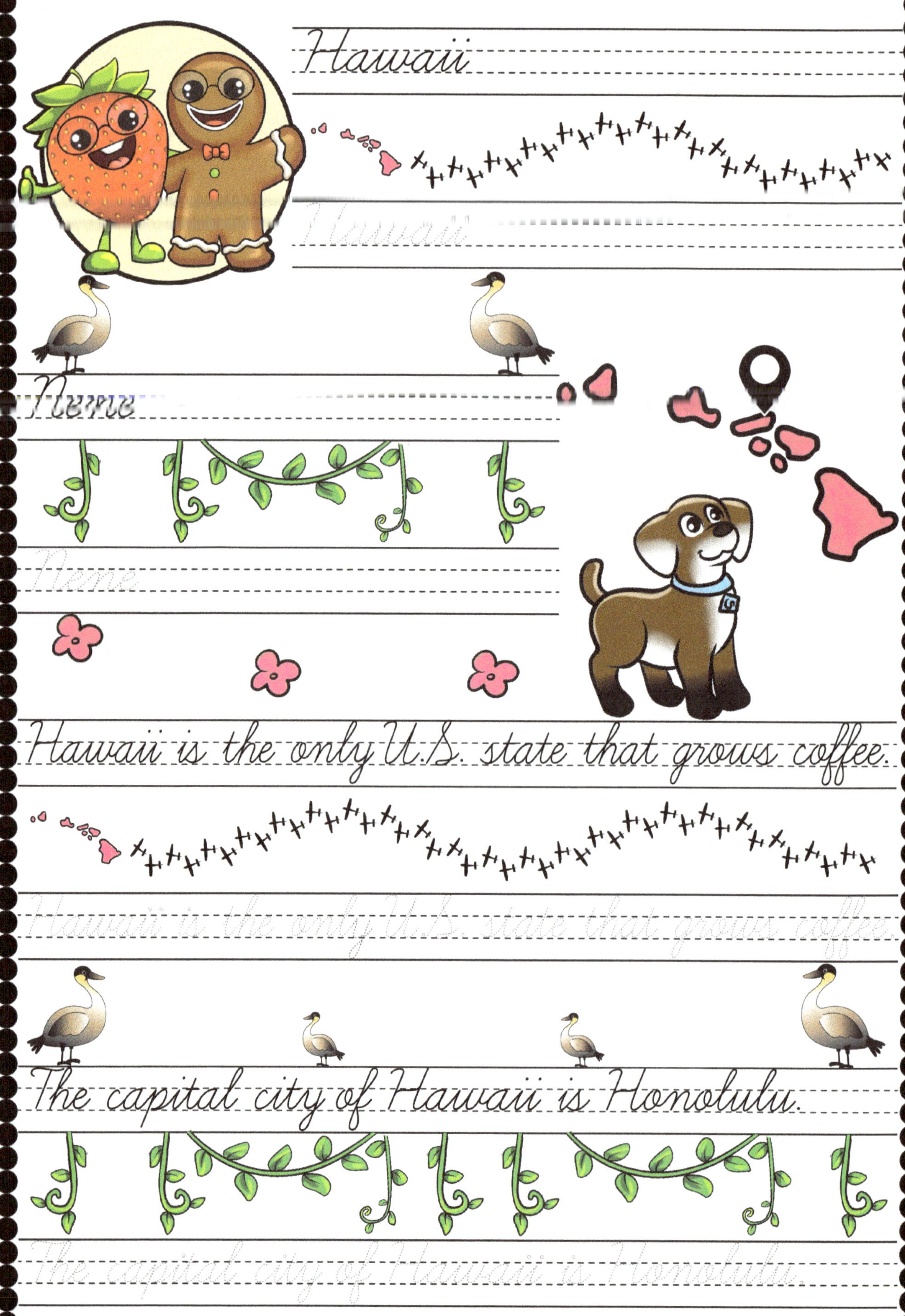

Hawaii

Hawaii

Name

Nene

Hawaii is the only U.S. state that grows coffee.

Hawaii is the only U.S. state that grows coffee.

The capital city of Hawaii is Honolulu.

The capital city of Hawaii is Honolulu.

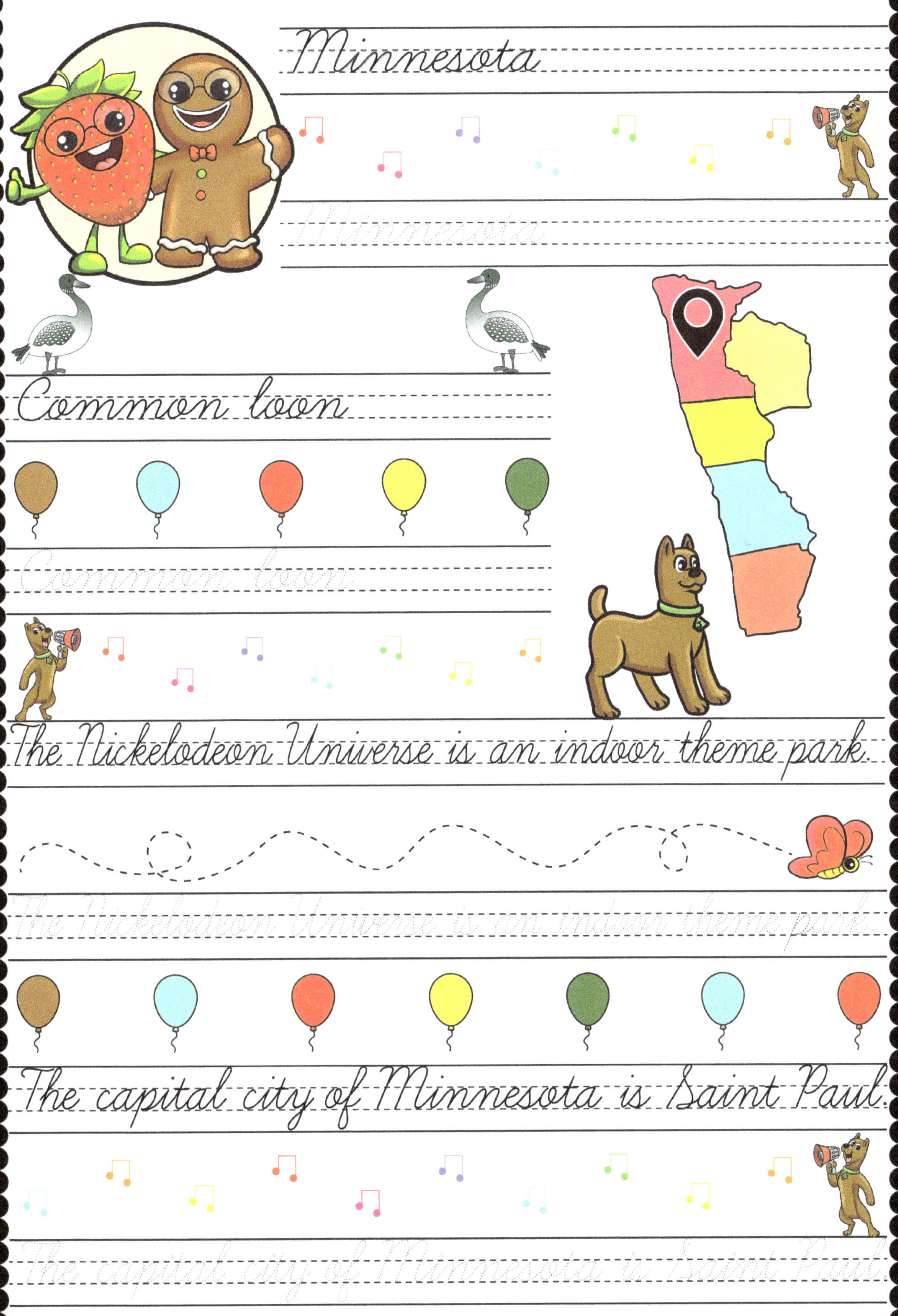

Minnesota

Common loon

The Nickelodeon Universe is an indoor theme park.

The capital city of Minnesota is Saint Paul.

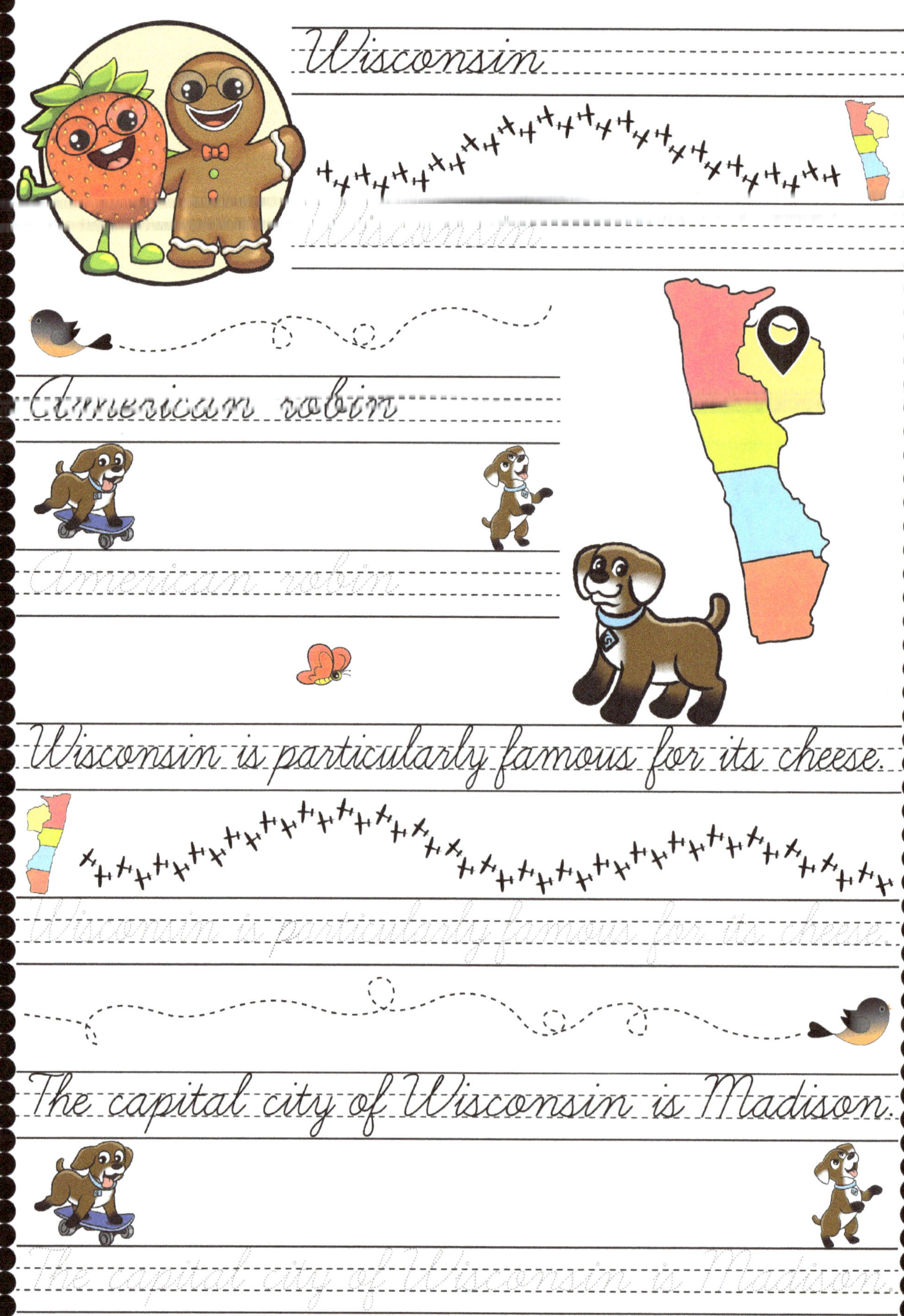

Wisconsin

American robin

Wisconsin is particularly famous for its cheese.

The capital city of Wisconsin is Madison.

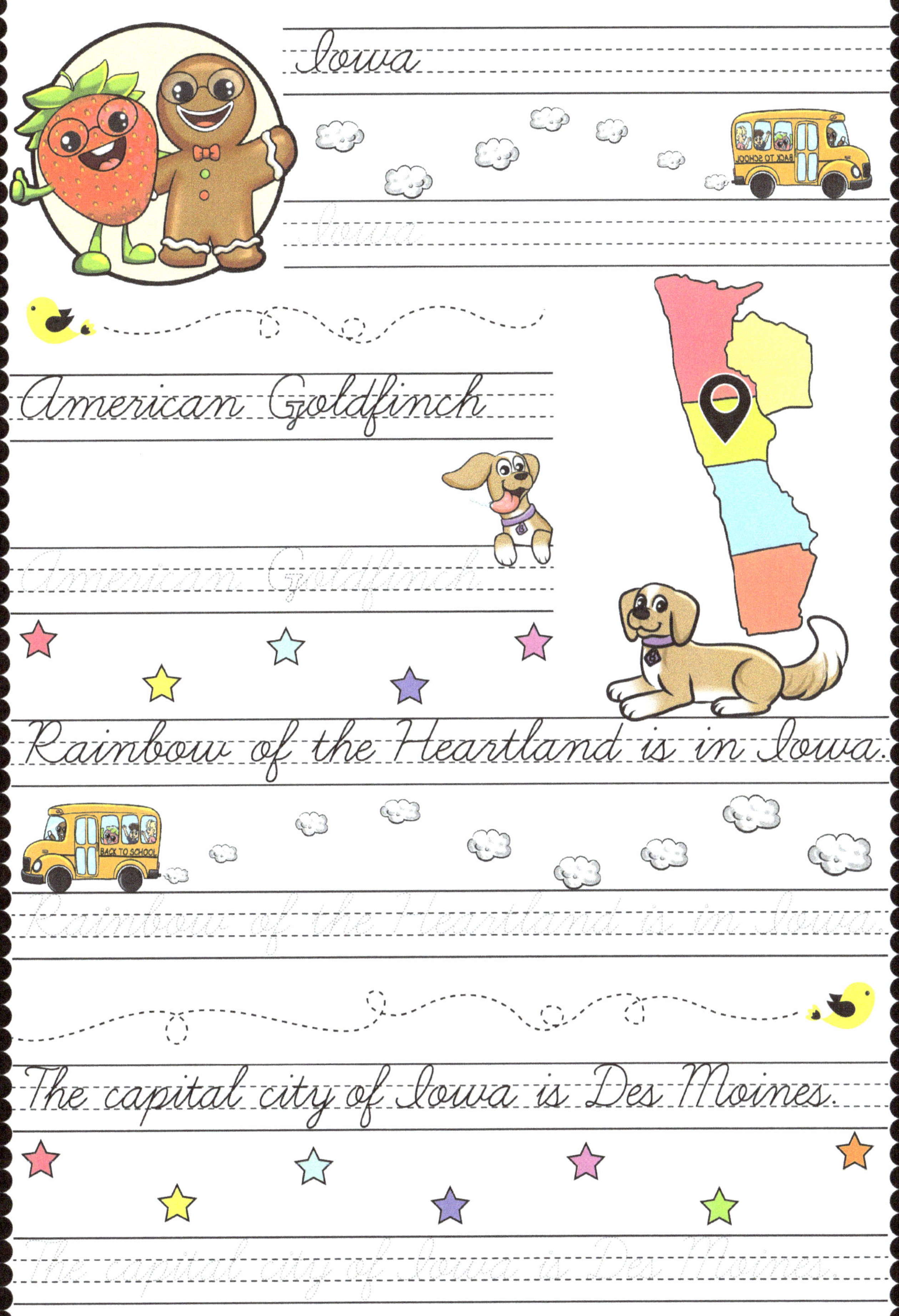

Iowa

Iowa

American Goldfinch

American Goldfinch

Rainbow of the Heartland is in Iowa.

Rainbow of the Heartland is in Iowa.

The capital city of Iowa is Des Moines.

The capital city of Iowa is Des Moines.

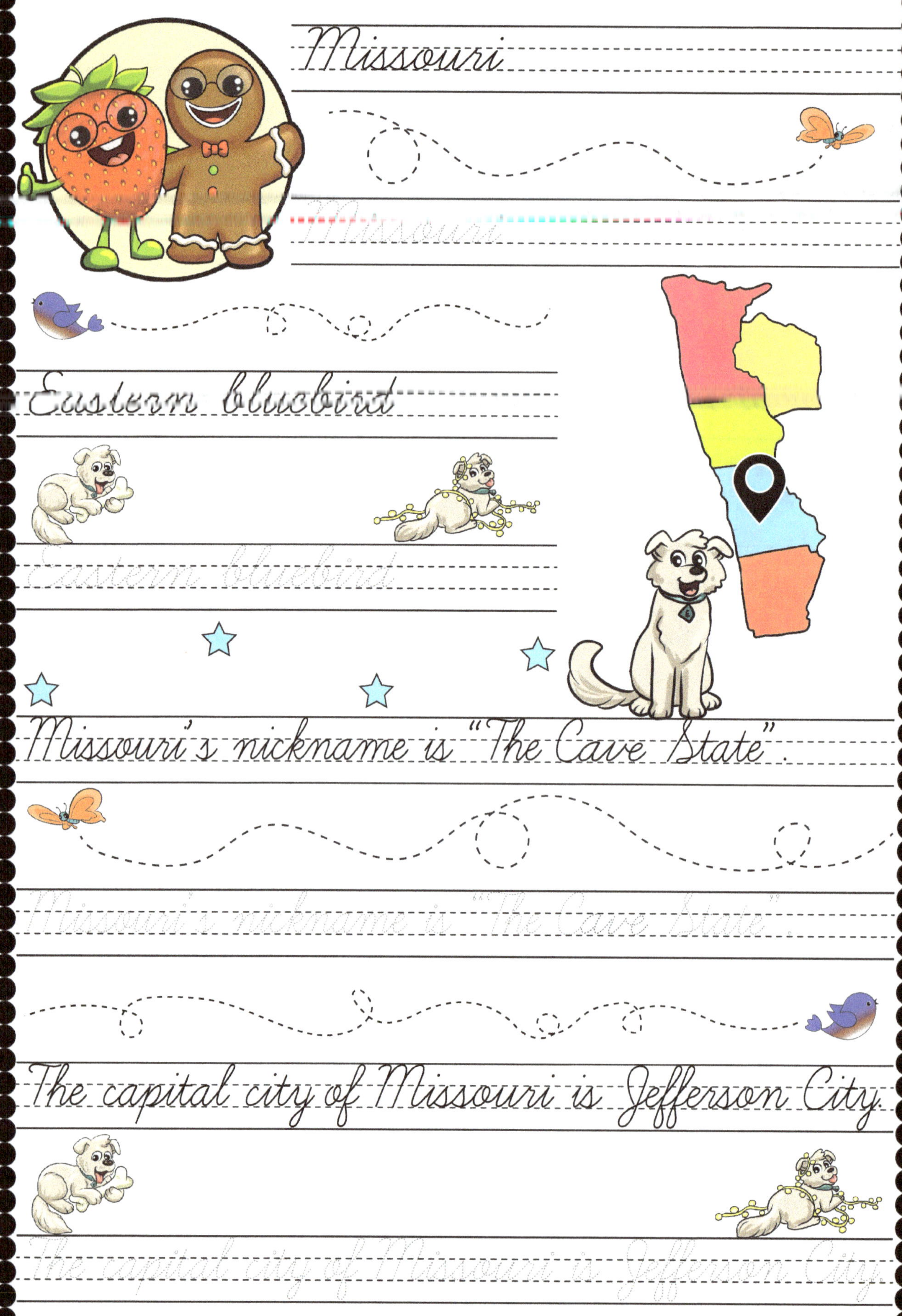

Missouri

Missouri

Eastern bluebird

Eastern bluebird

Missouri's nickname is "The Cave State"

Missouri's nickname is "The Cave State"

The capital city of Missouri is Jefferson City.

The capital city of Missouri is Jefferson City.

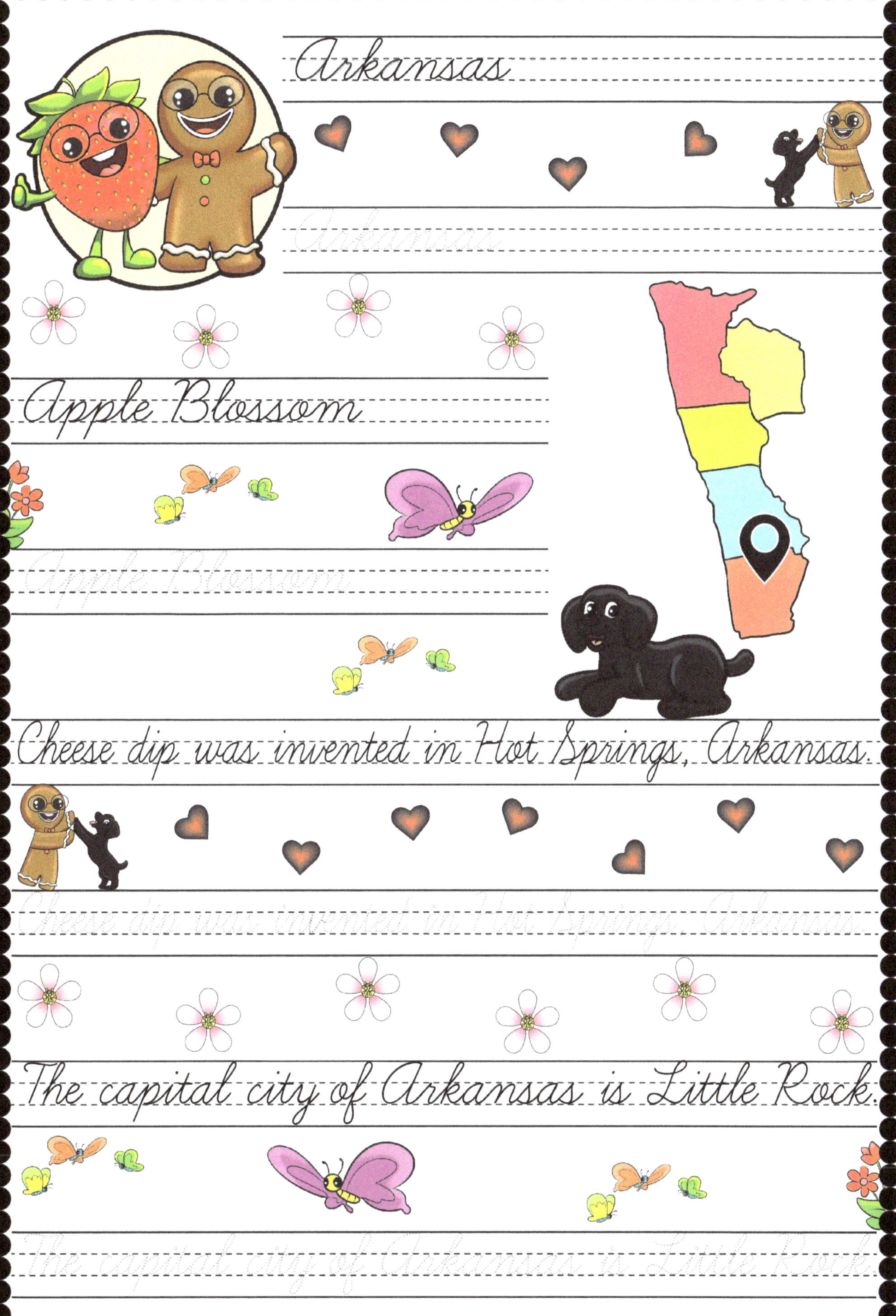

Arkansas

Apple Blossom

Cheese dip was invented in Hot Springs, Arkansas.

The capital city of Arkansas is Little Rock.

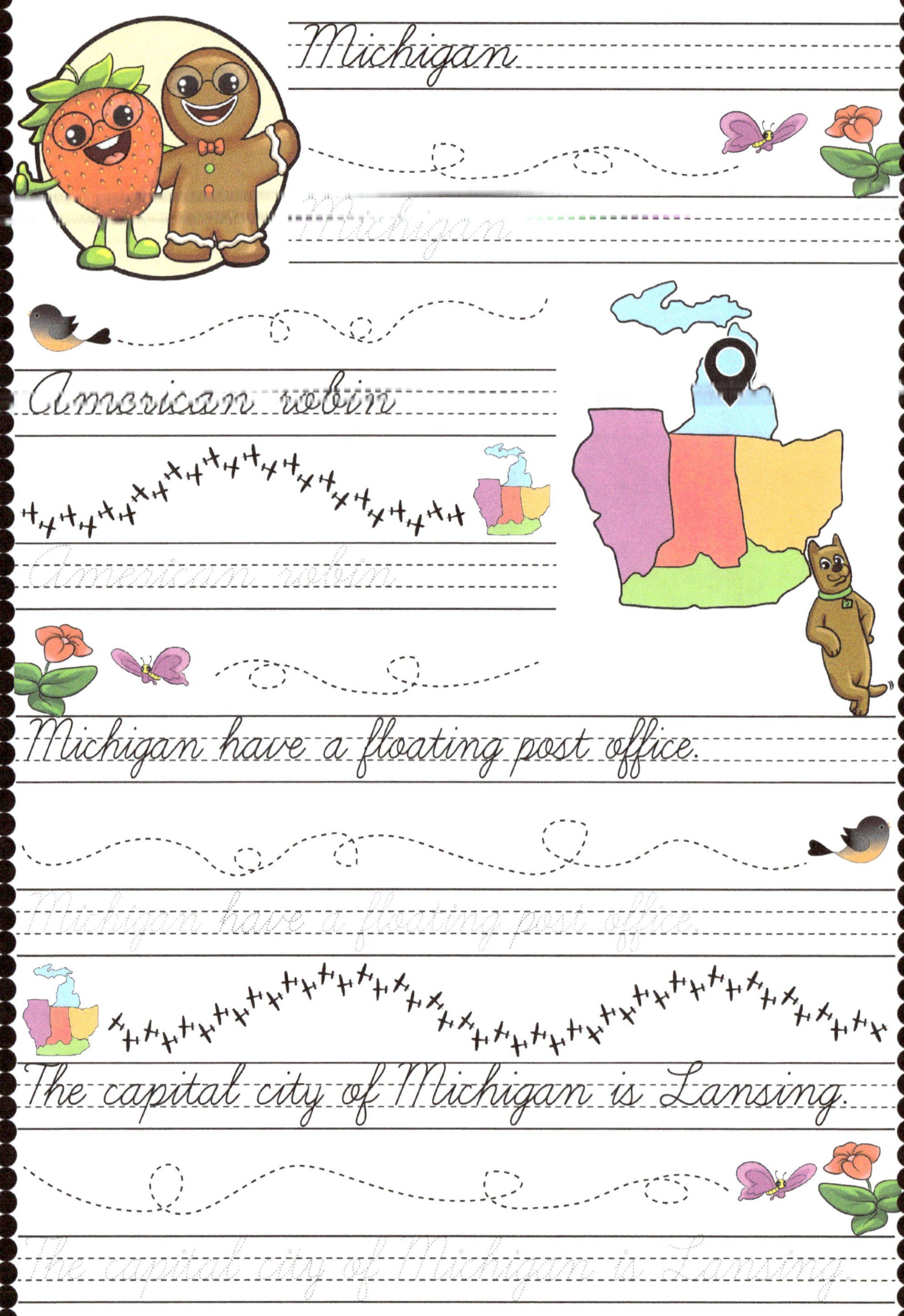

Michigan

Michigan

American robin

American robin

Michigan have a floating post office.

Michigan have a floating post office.

The capital city of Michigan is Lansing.

The capital city of Michigan is Lansing.

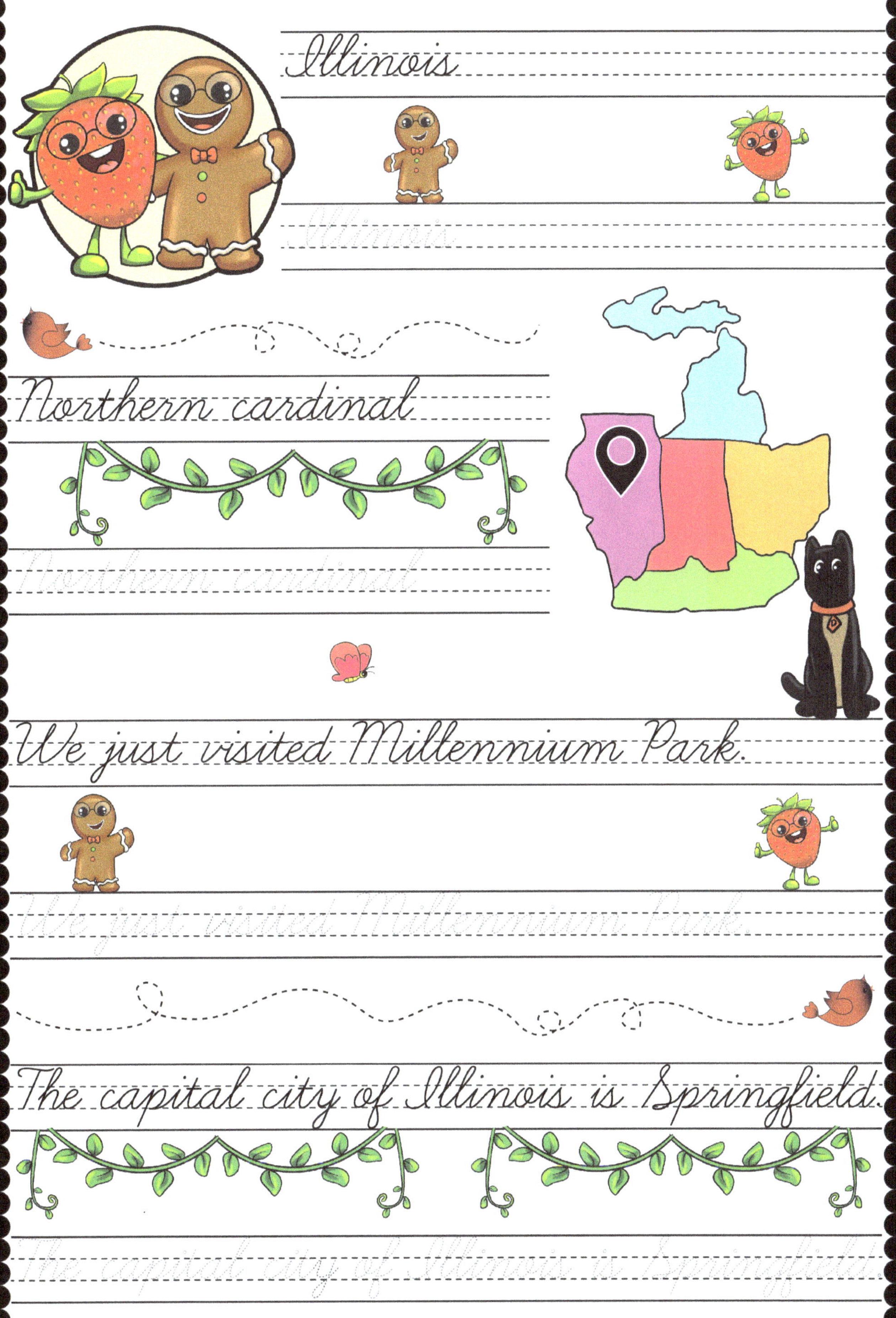

Illinois

Illinois

Northern cardinal

Northern cardinal

We just visited Millennium Park.

We just visited Millennium Park.

The capital city of Illinois is Springfield.

The capital city of Illinois is Springfield.

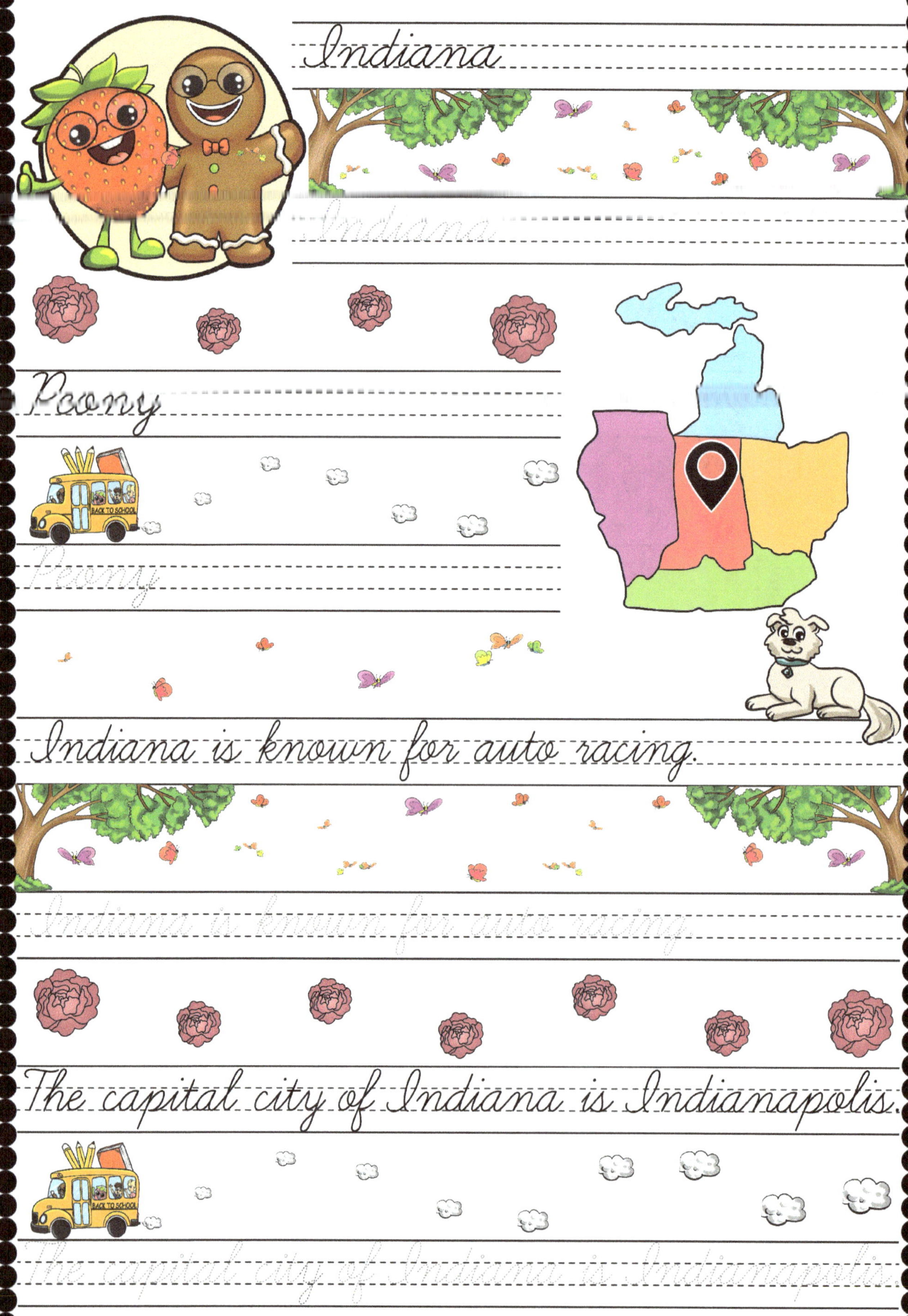

Indiana
Indiana
Peony
Peony
Indiana is known for auto racing.
Indiana is known for auto racing.
The capital city of Indiana is Indianapolis.
The capital city of Indiana is Indianapolis.

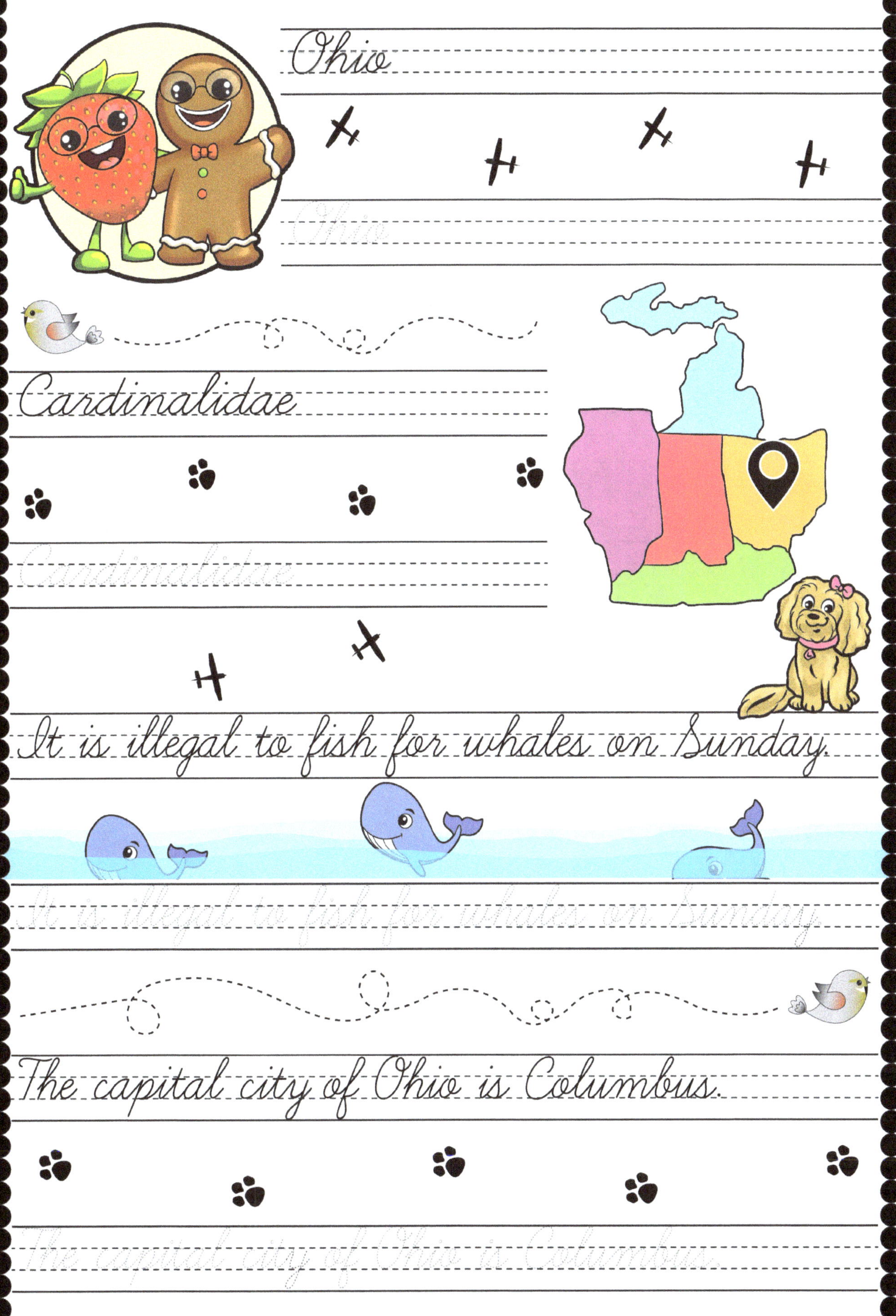

Ohio

Ohio

Cardinalidae

Cardinalidae

It is illegal to fish for whales on Sunday.

It is illegal to fish for whales on Sunday.

The capital city of Ohio is Columbus.

The capital city of Ohio is Columbus.

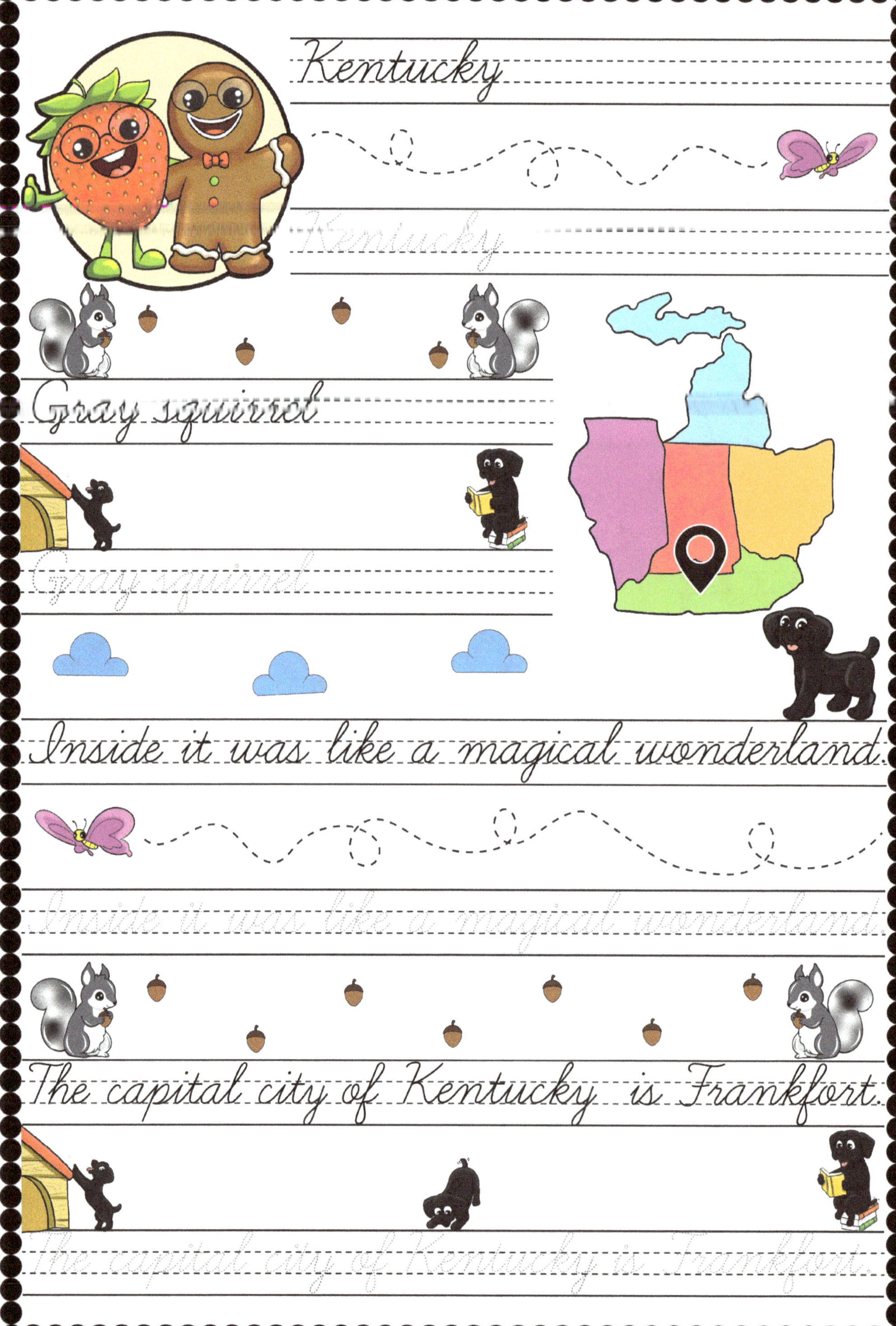

Kentucky
Kentucky
Gray squirrel
Gray squirrel
Inside it was like a magical wonderland.
Inside it was like a magical wonderland.
The capital city of Kentucky is Frankfort.
The capital city of Kentucky is Frankfort.

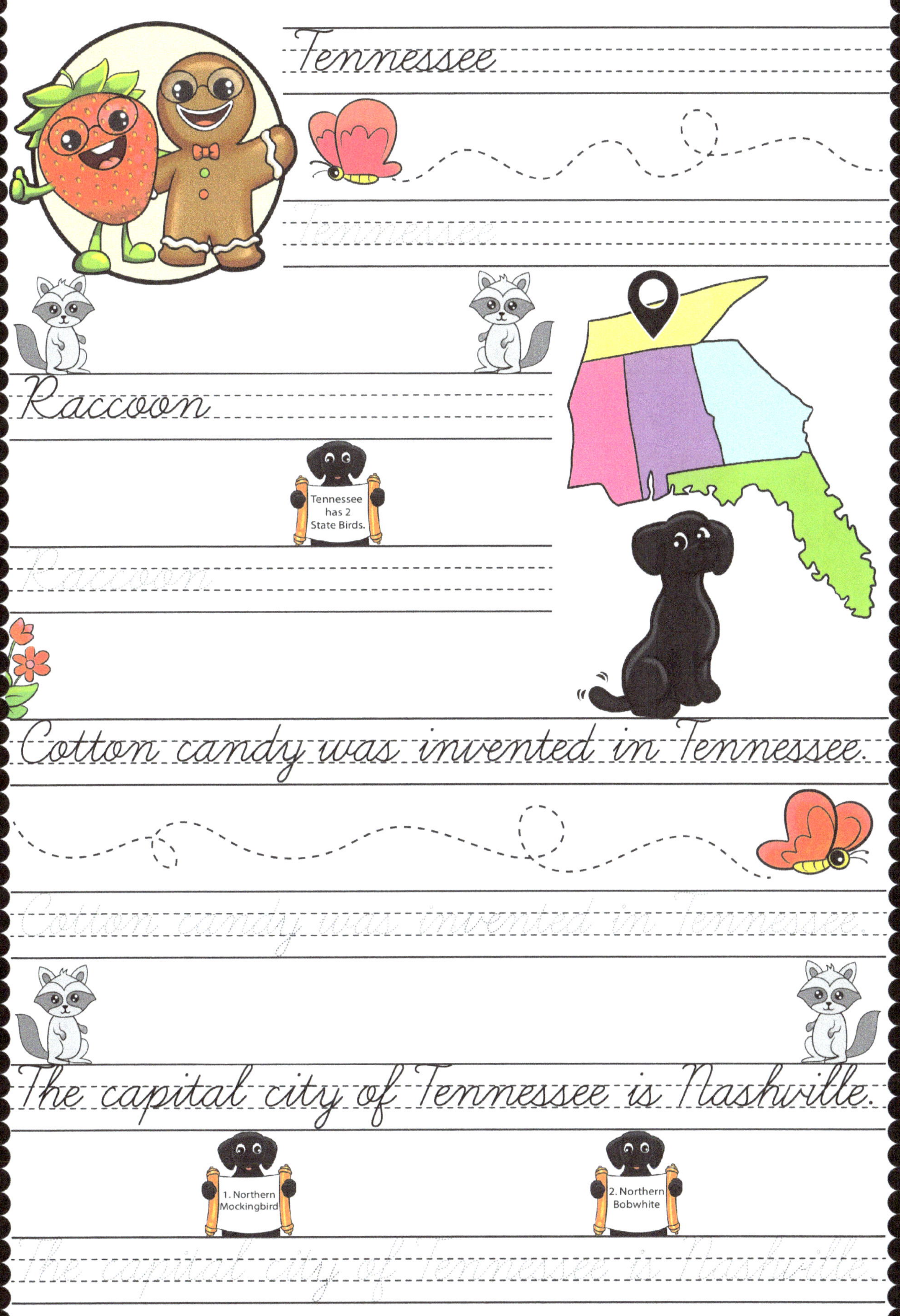

Tennessee
Tennessee

Raccoon
Raccoon

Tennessee has 2 State Birds.

Cotton candy was invented in Tennessee.
Cotton candy was invented in Tennessee.

The capital city of Tennessee is Nashville.
The capital city of Tennessee is Nashville.

1. Northern Mockingbird
2. Northern Bobwhite

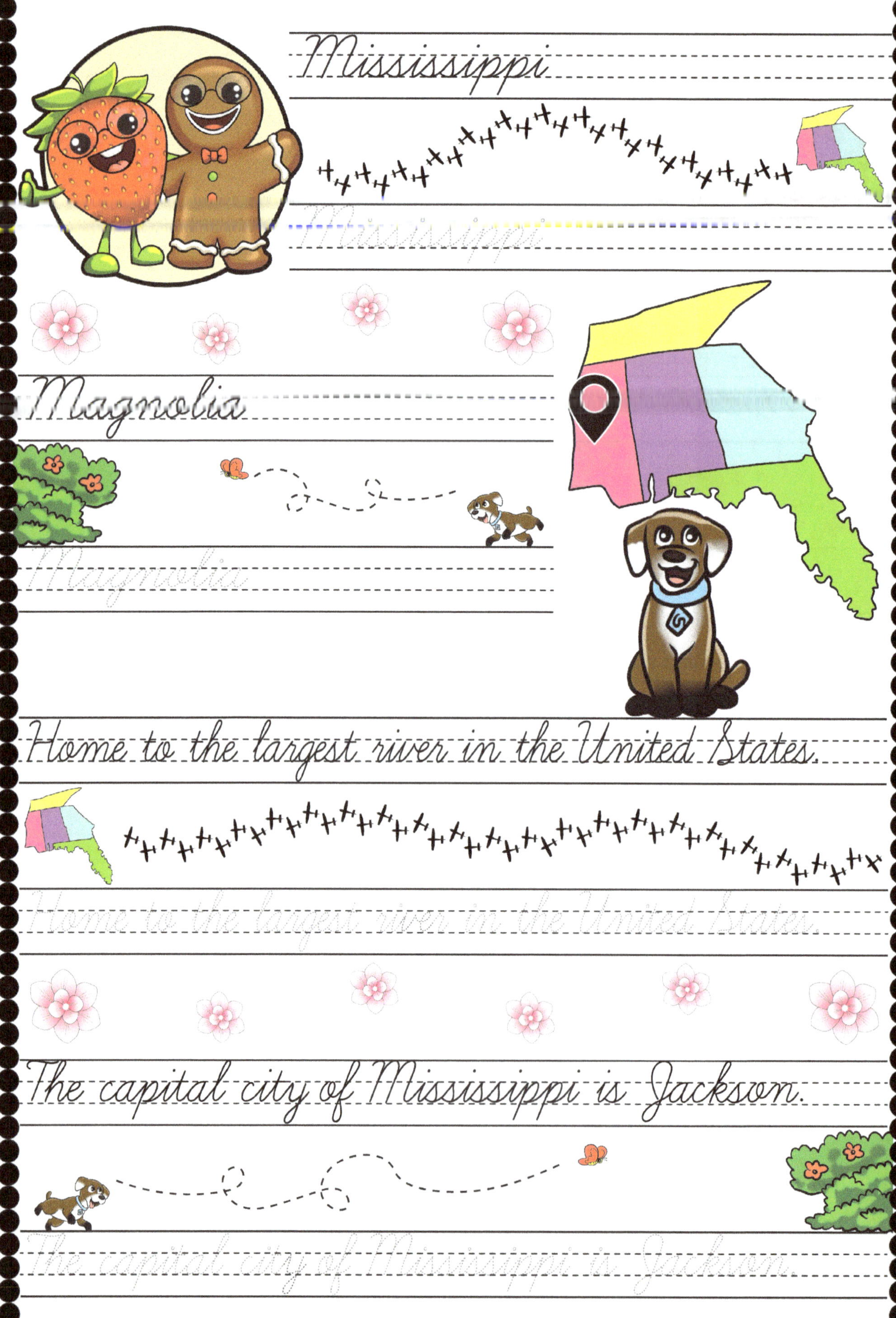

Mississippi

Mississippi

Magnolia

Magnolia

Home to the largest river in the United States.

Home to the largest river in the United States.

The capital city of Mississippi is Jackson.

The capital city of Mississippi is Jackson.

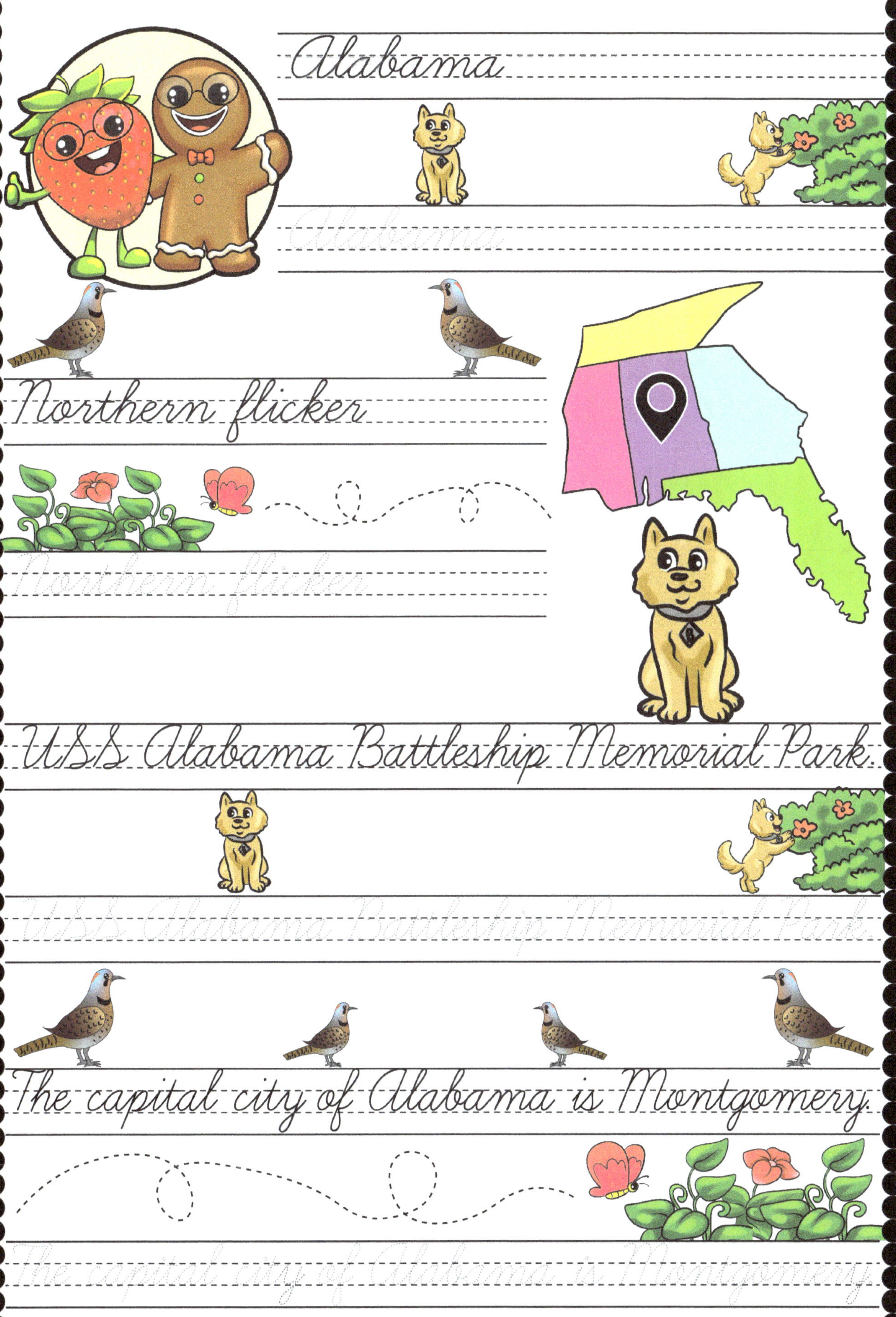

Alabama

Alabama

Northern flicker

Northern flicker

U.S.S. Alabama Battleship Memorial Park

U.S.S. Alabama Battleship Memorial Park

The capital city of Alabama is Montgomery.

The capital city of Alabama is Montgomery.

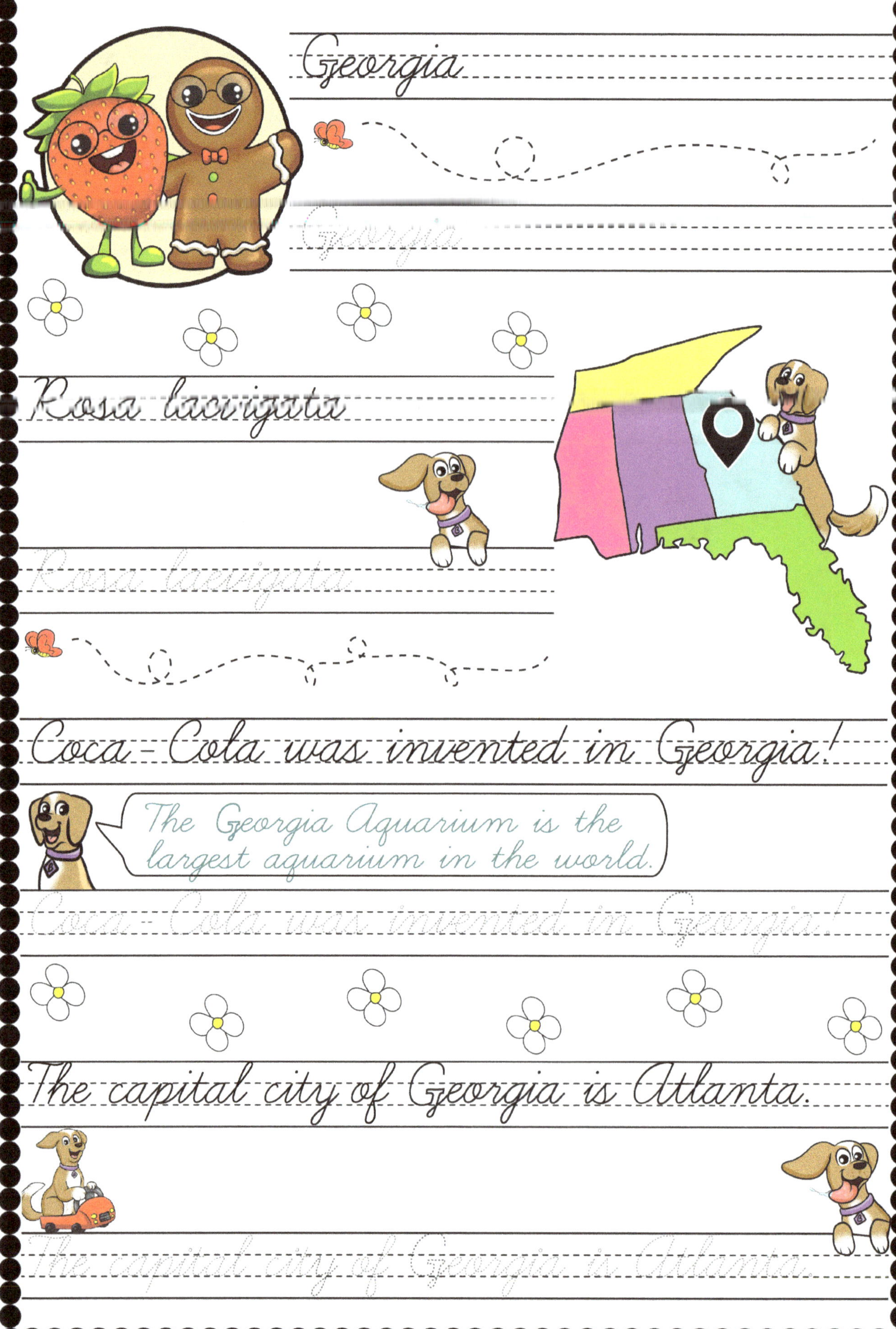

Georgia

Georgia

Rosa laevigata

Rosa laevigata

Coca-Cola was invented in Georgia!

Coca-Cola was invented in Georgia!

The capital city of Georgia is Atlanta.

The capital city of Georgia is Atlanta.

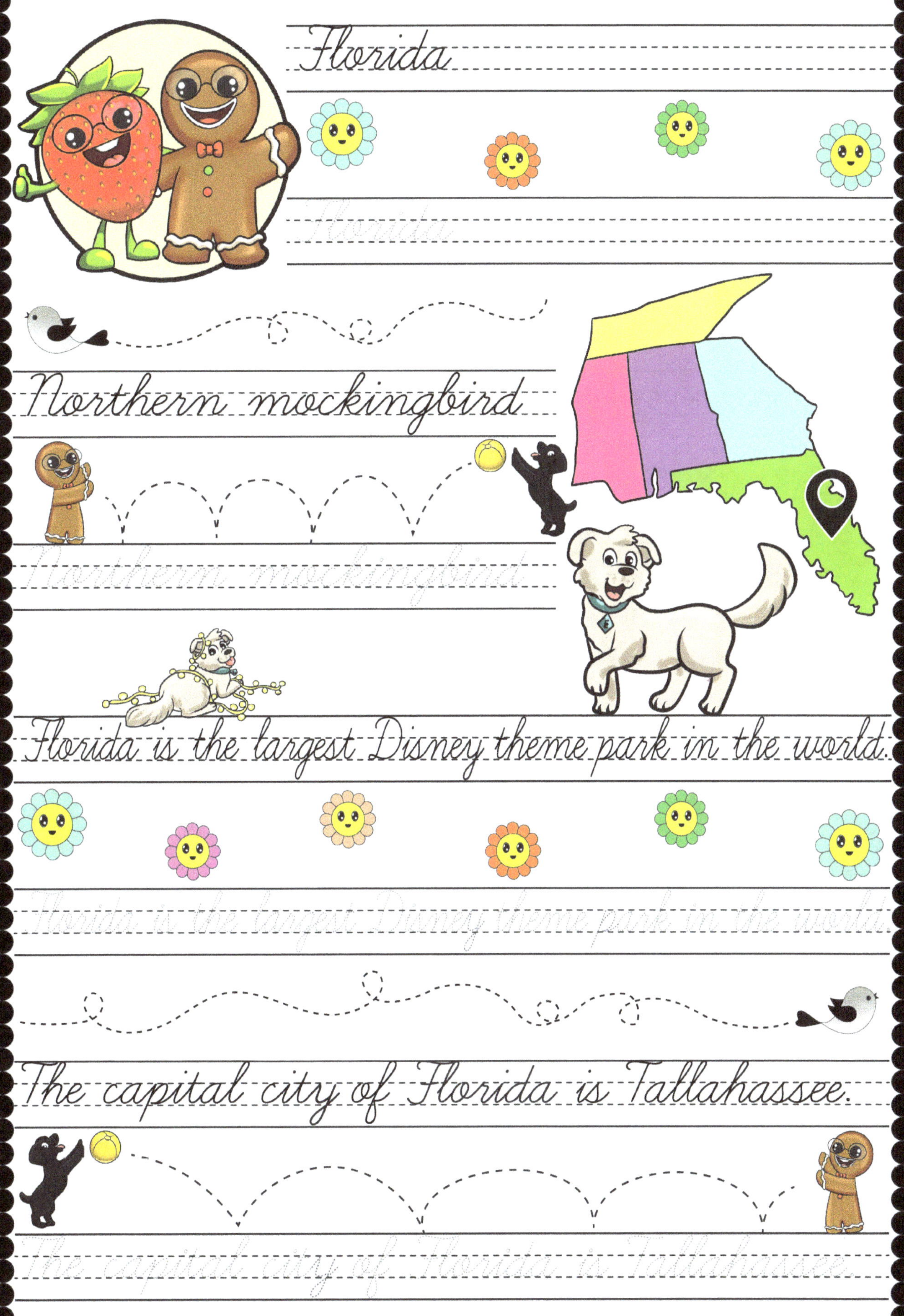

Florida

Florida

Northern mockingbird

Northern mockingbird

Florida is the largest Disney theme park in the world.

Florida is the largest Disney theme park in the world.

The capital city of Florida is Tallahassee.

The capital city of Florida is Tallahassee.

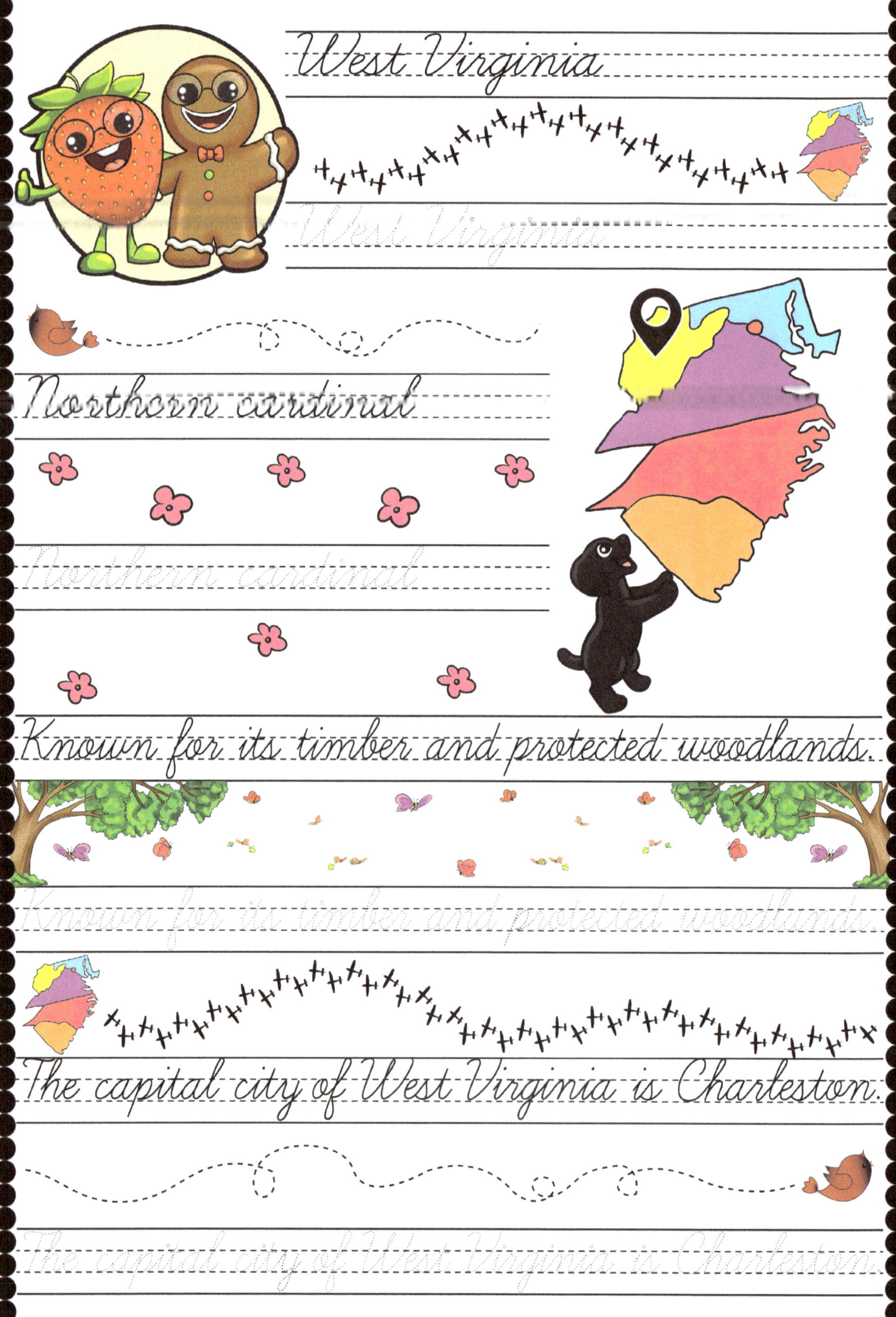

West Virginia

West Virginia

Northern cardinal

Northern cardinal

Known for its timber and protected woodlands.

Known for its timber and protected woodlands.

The capital city of West Virginia is Charleston.

The capital city of West Virginia is Charleston.

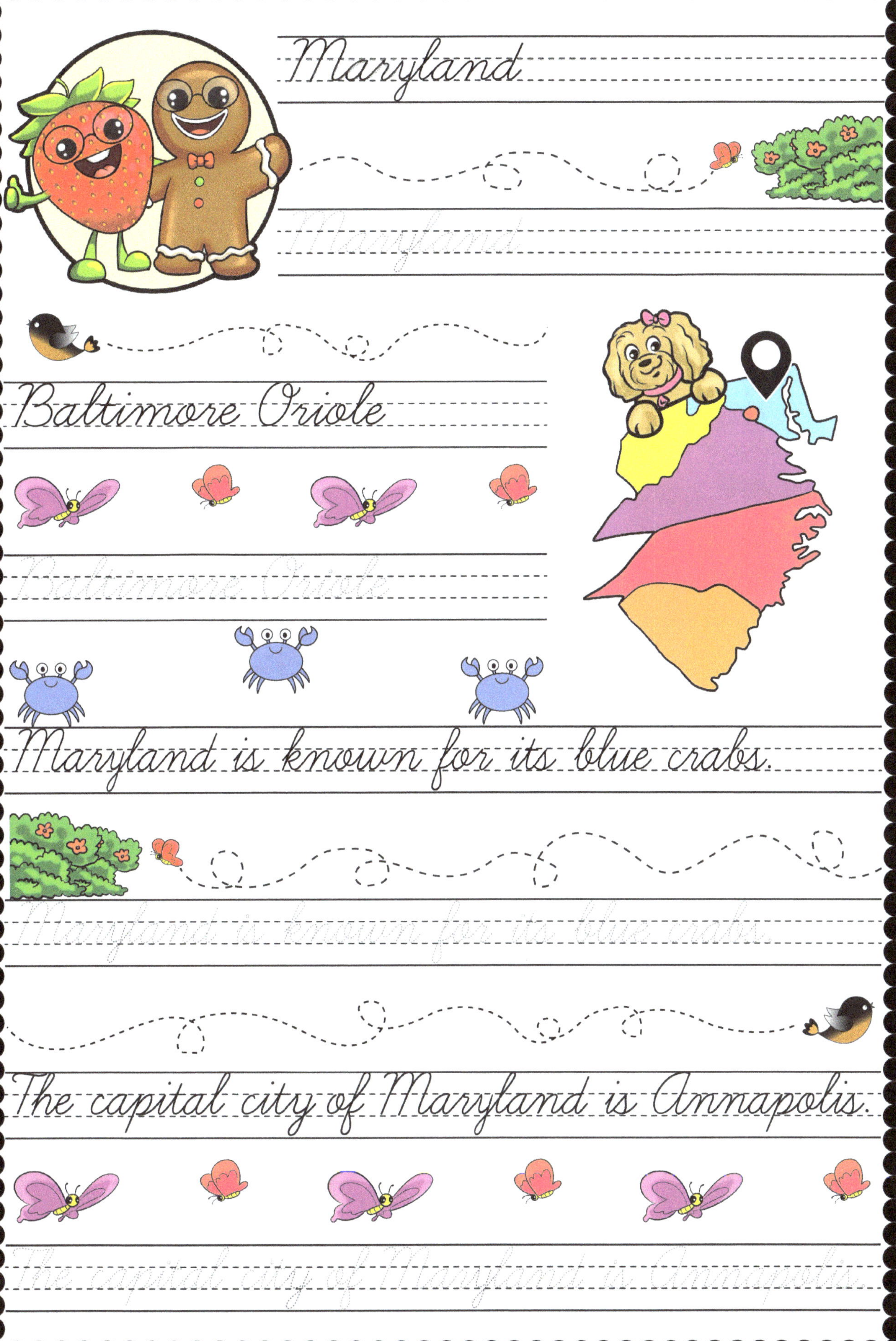

Maryland

Maryland

Baltimore Oriole

Baltimore Oriole

Maryland is known for its blue crabs.

Maryland is known for its blue crabs.

The capital city of Maryland is Annapolis.

The capital city of Maryland is Annapolis.

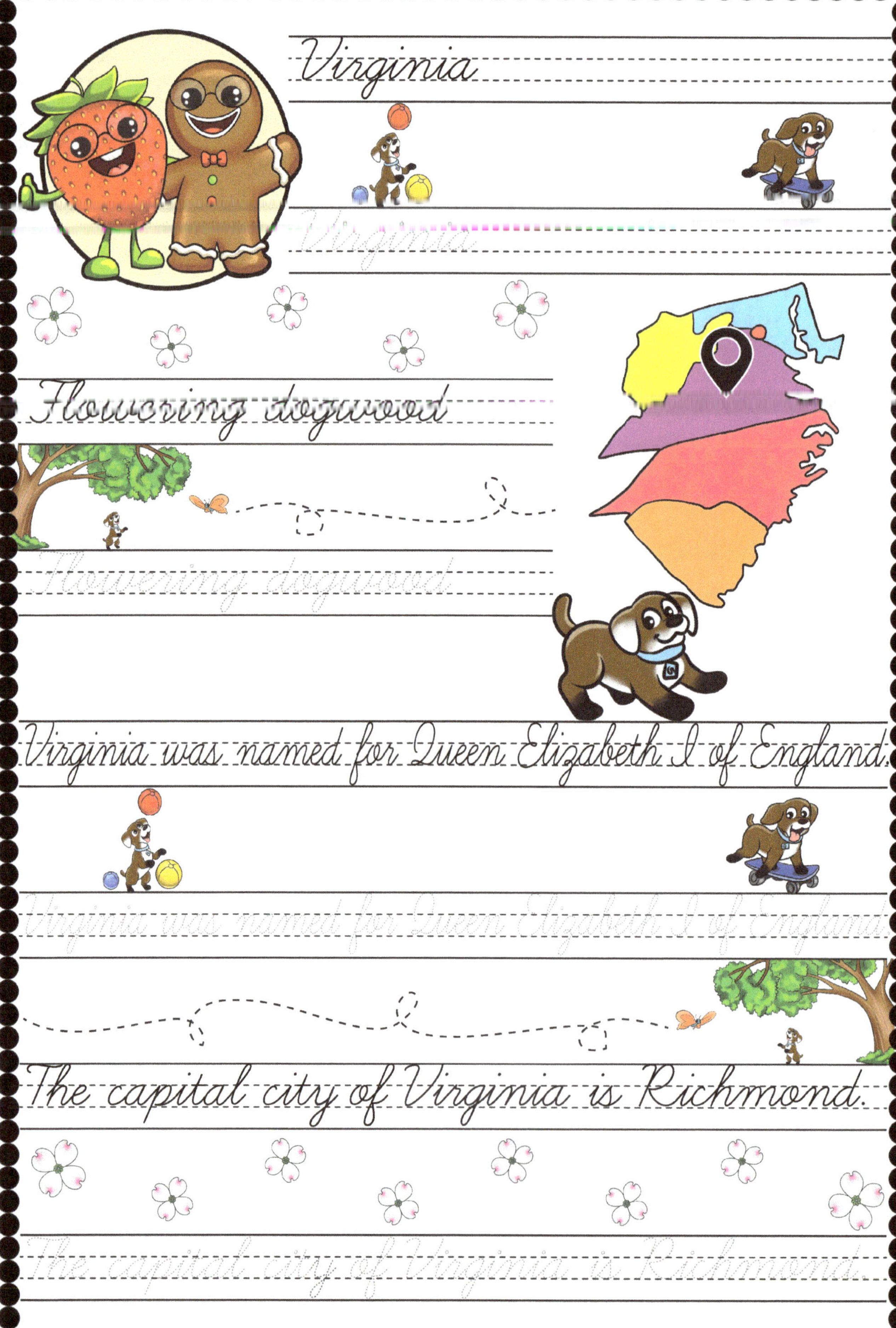

Virginia

Virginia

Flowering dogwood

Flowering dogwood

Virginia was named for Queen Elizabeth I of England.

Virginia was named for Queen Elizabeth I of England.

The capital city of Virginia is Richmond.

The capital city of Virginia is Richmond.

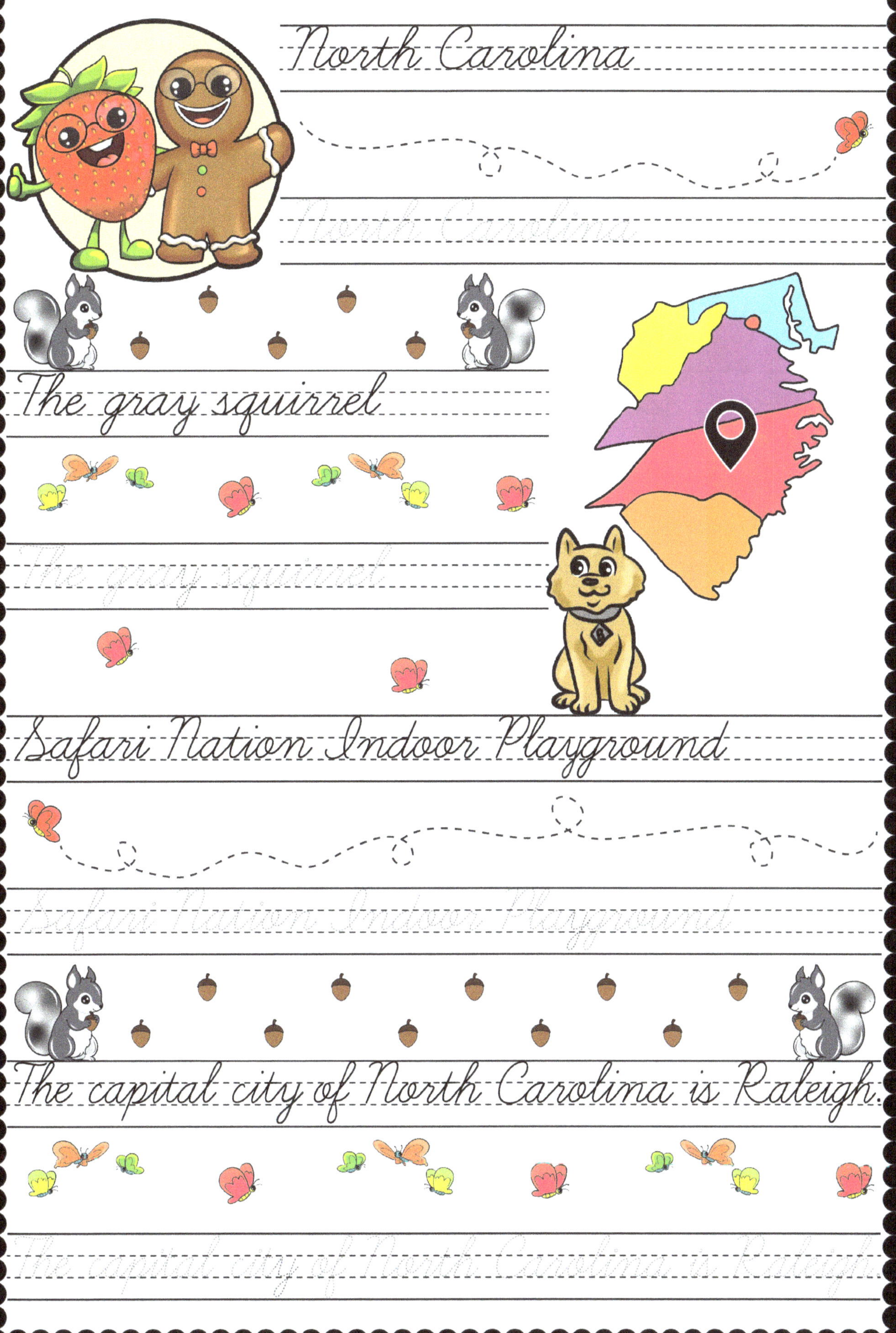

North Carolina
North Carolina
The gray squirrel
The gray squirrel
Safari Nation Indoor Playground
Safari Nation Indoor Playground
The capital city of North Carolina is Raleigh.
The capital city of North Carolina is Raleigh.

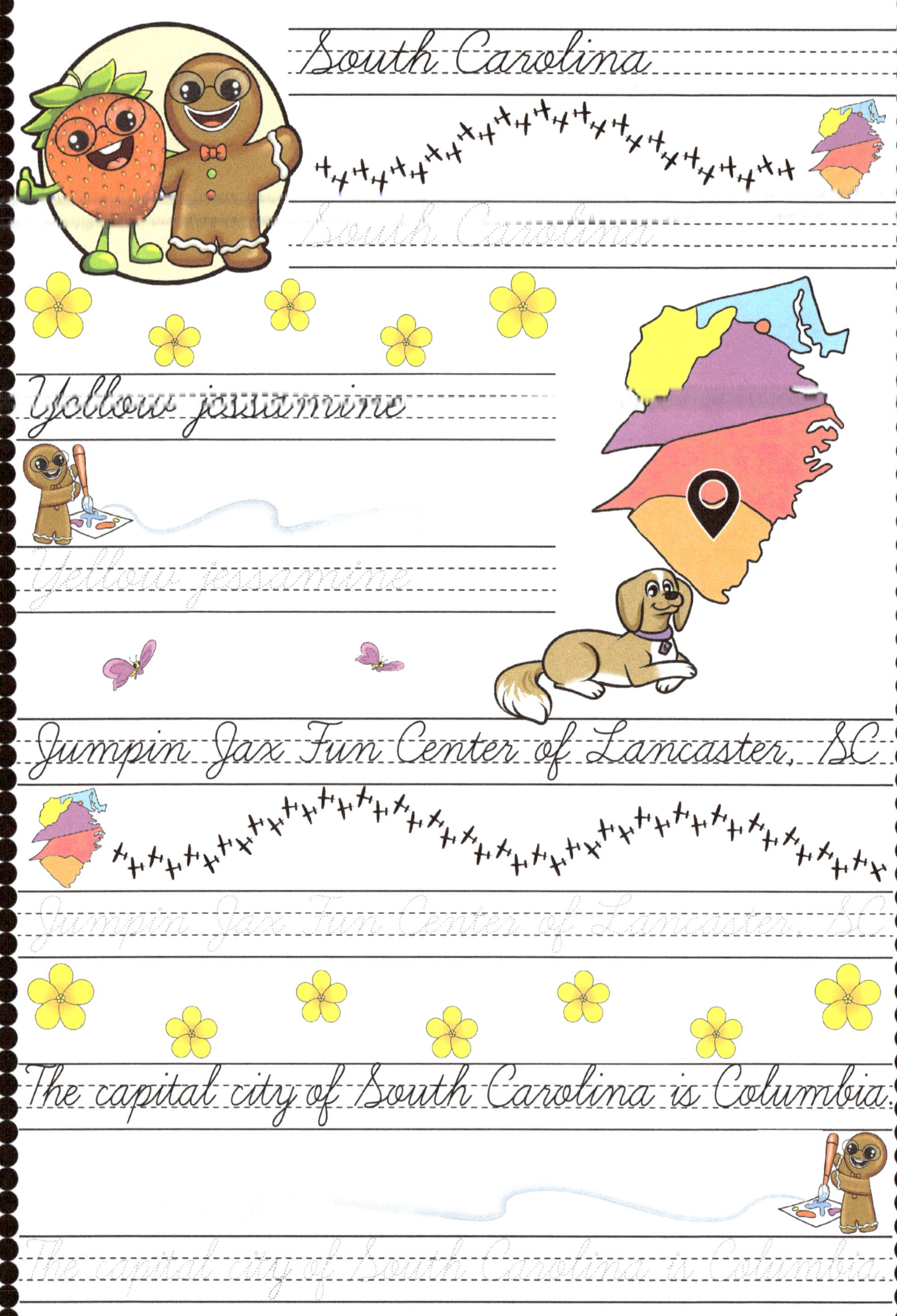

South Carolina

South Carolina

Yellow jessamine

Yellow jessamine

Jumpin Jax Fun Center of Lancaster, SC

Jumpin Jax Fun Center of Lancaster, SC

The capital city of South Carolina is Columbia.

The capital city of South Carolina is Columbia.

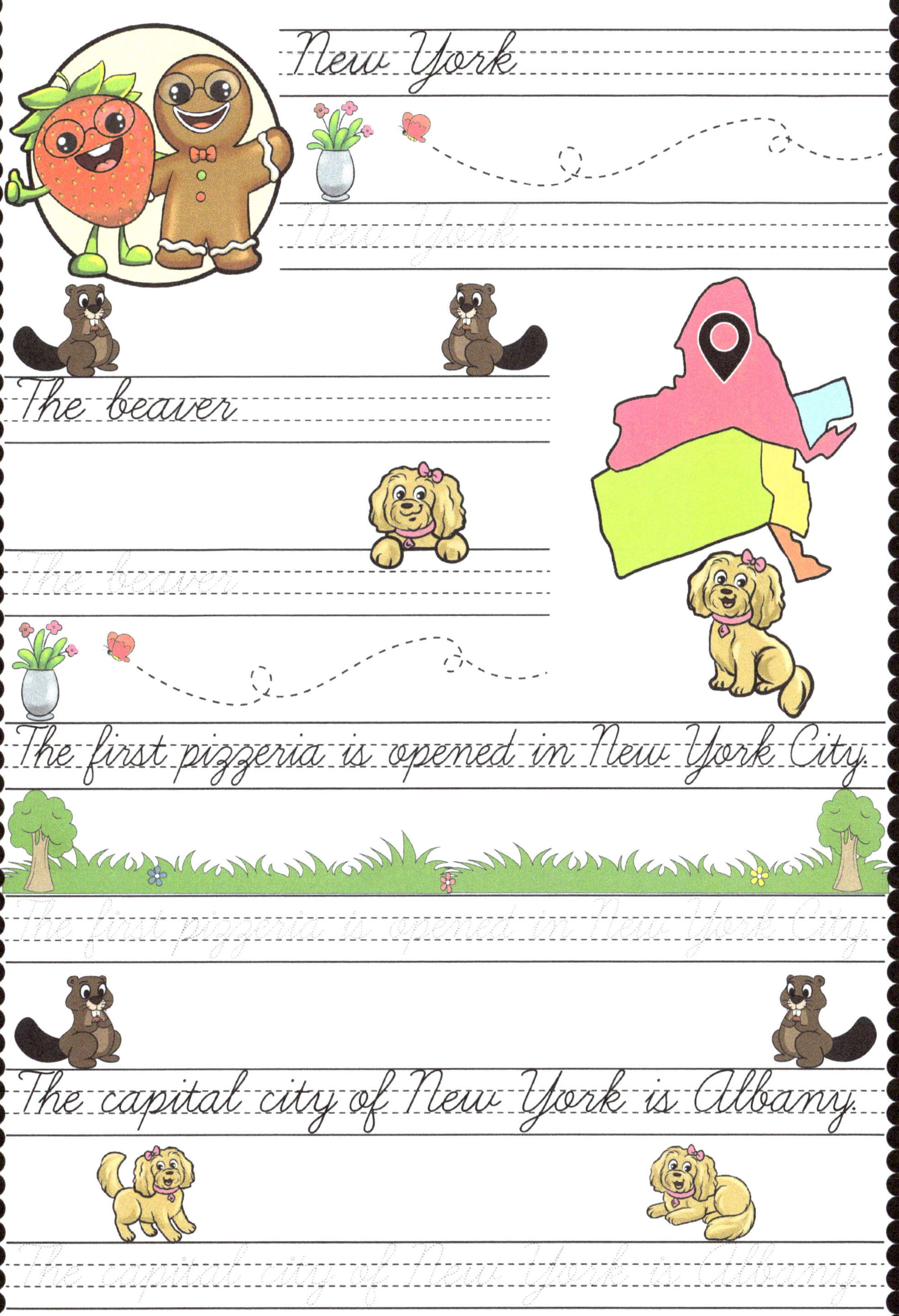

New York
New York
The beaver
The beaver
The first pizzeria is opened in New York City.
The first pizzeria is opened in New York City.
The capital city of New York is Albany.
The capital city of New York is Albany.

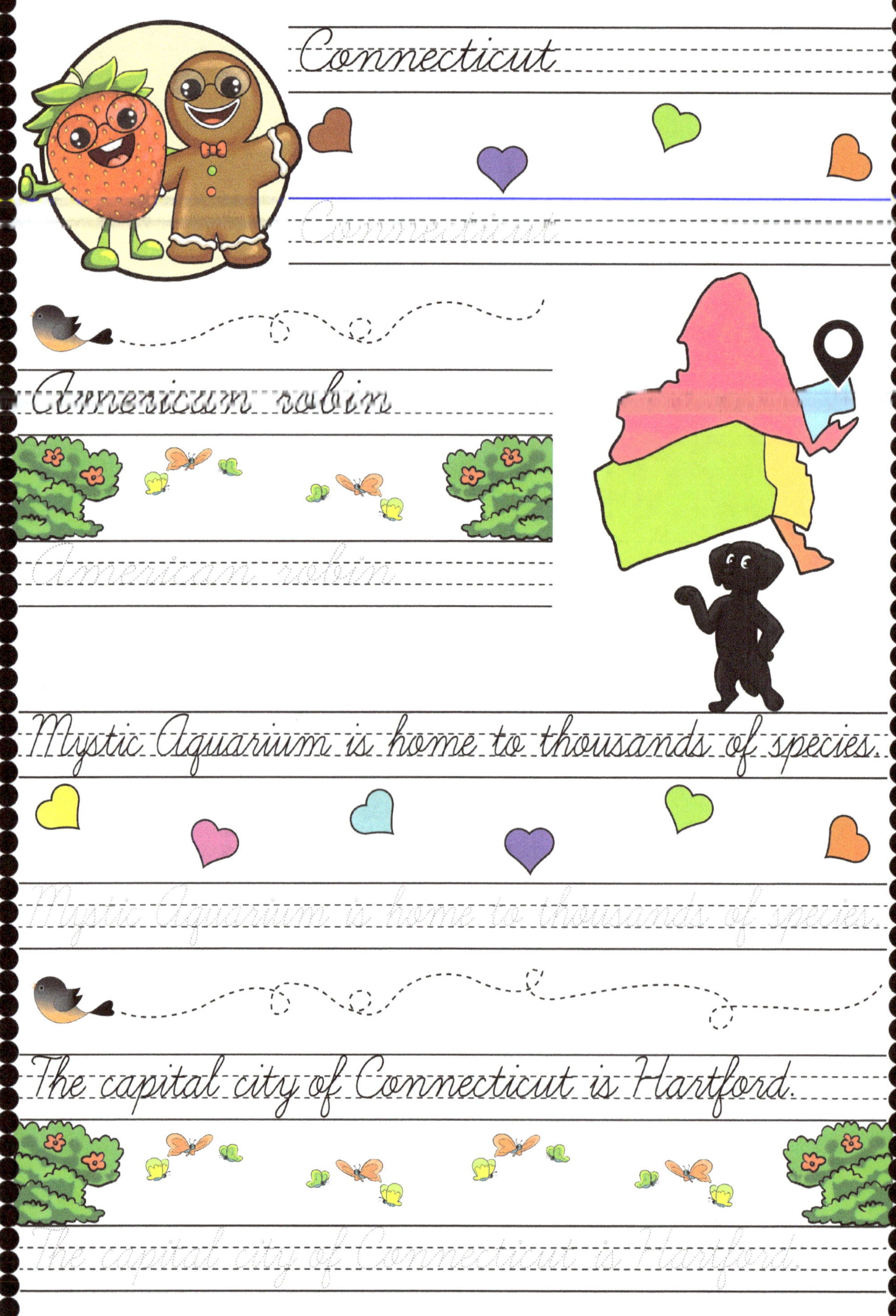

Connecticut

Connecticut

American robin

American robin

Mystic Aquarium is home to thousands of species.

Mystic Aquarium is home to thousands of species.

The capital city of Connecticut is Hartford.

The capital city of Connecticut is Hartford.

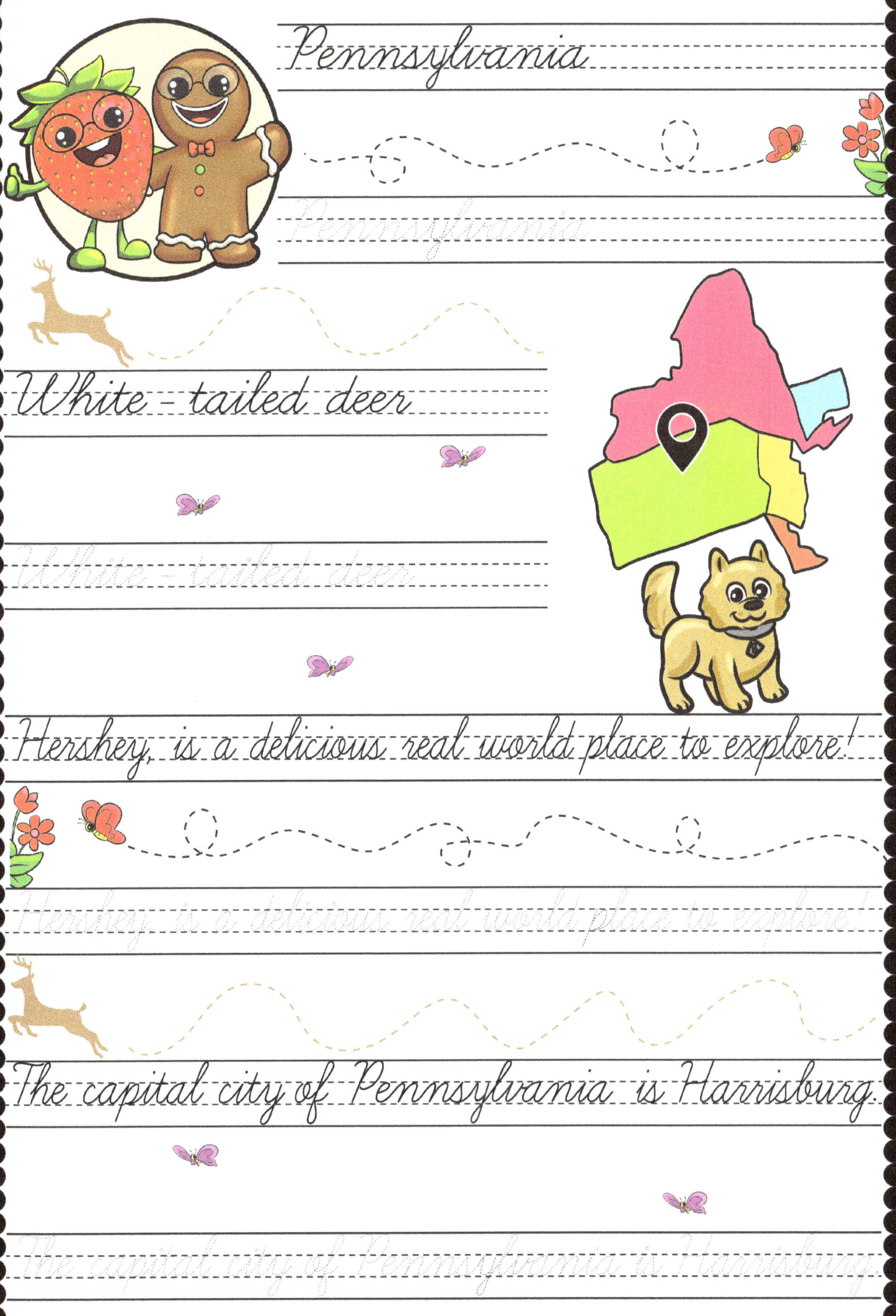

Pennsylvania

Pennsylvania

White - tailed deer

White - tailed deer

Hershey, is a delicious real world place to explore!

Hershey, is a delicious real world place to explore!

The capital city of Pennsylvania is Harrisburg.

The capital city of Pennsylvania is Harrisburg.

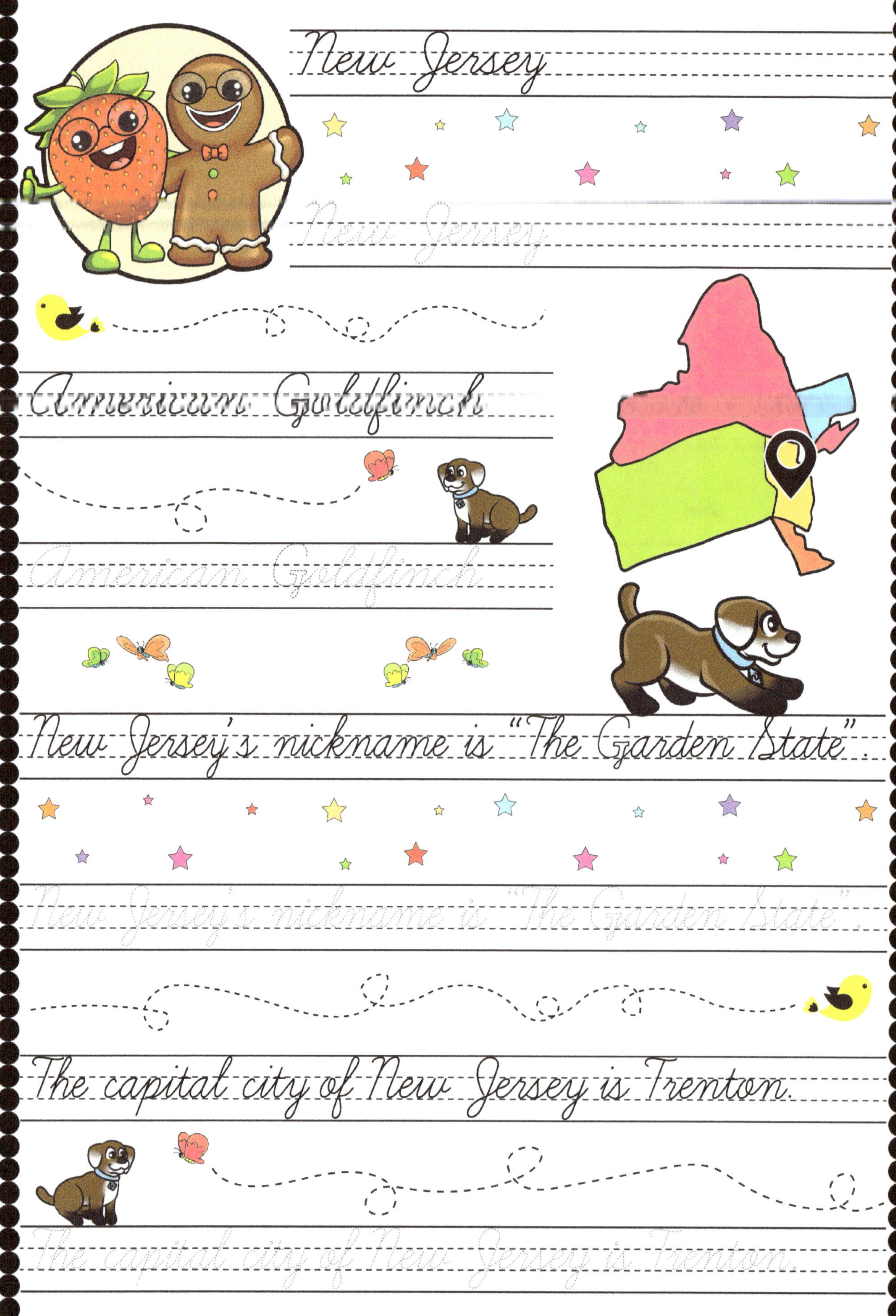

New Jersey

New Jersey

American Goldfinch

American Goldfinch

New Jersey's nickname is "The Garden State".

New Jersey's nickname is "The Garden State".

The capital city of New Jersey is Trenton.

The capital city of New Jersey is Trenton.

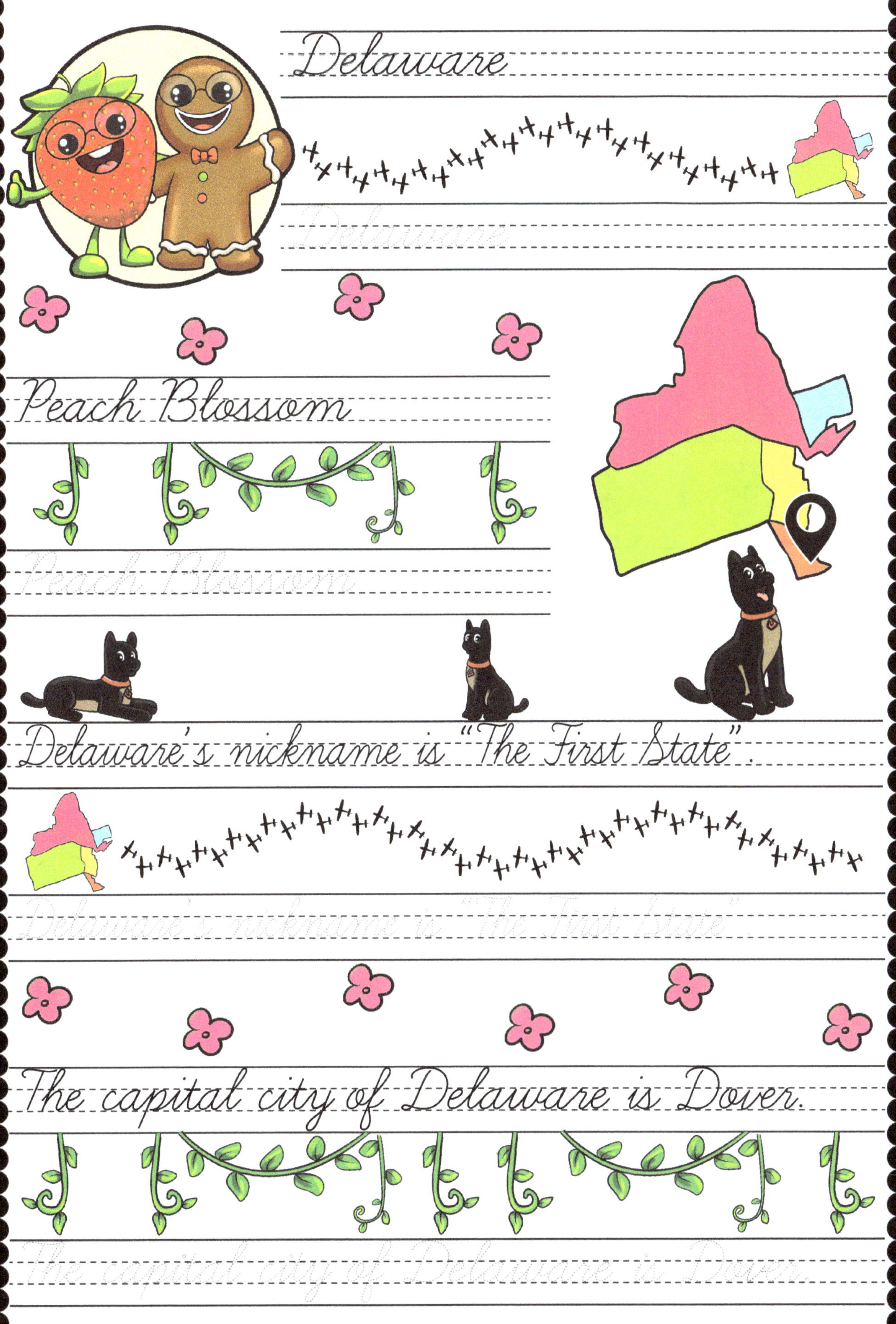

Delaware
Delaware
Peach Blossom
Peach Blossom
Delaware's nickname is "The First State".
Delaware's nickname is "The First State"
The capital city of Delaware is Dover.
The capital city of Delaware is Dover.

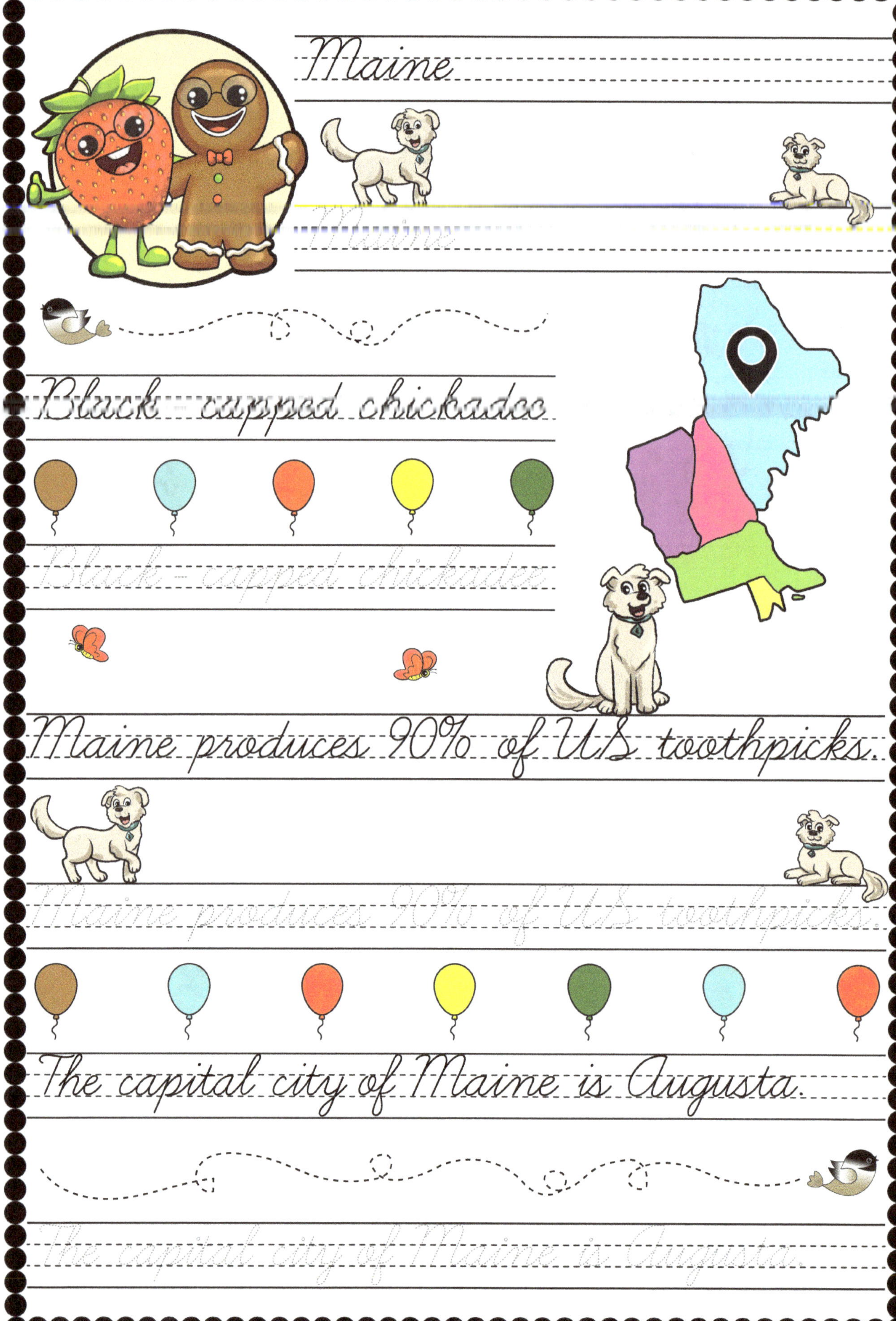

Maine

Maine

Black - capped chickadee

Black - capped chickadee

Maine produces 90% of US toothpicks.

Maine produces 90% of US toothpicks.

The capital city of Maine is Augusta.

The capital city of Maine is Augusta.

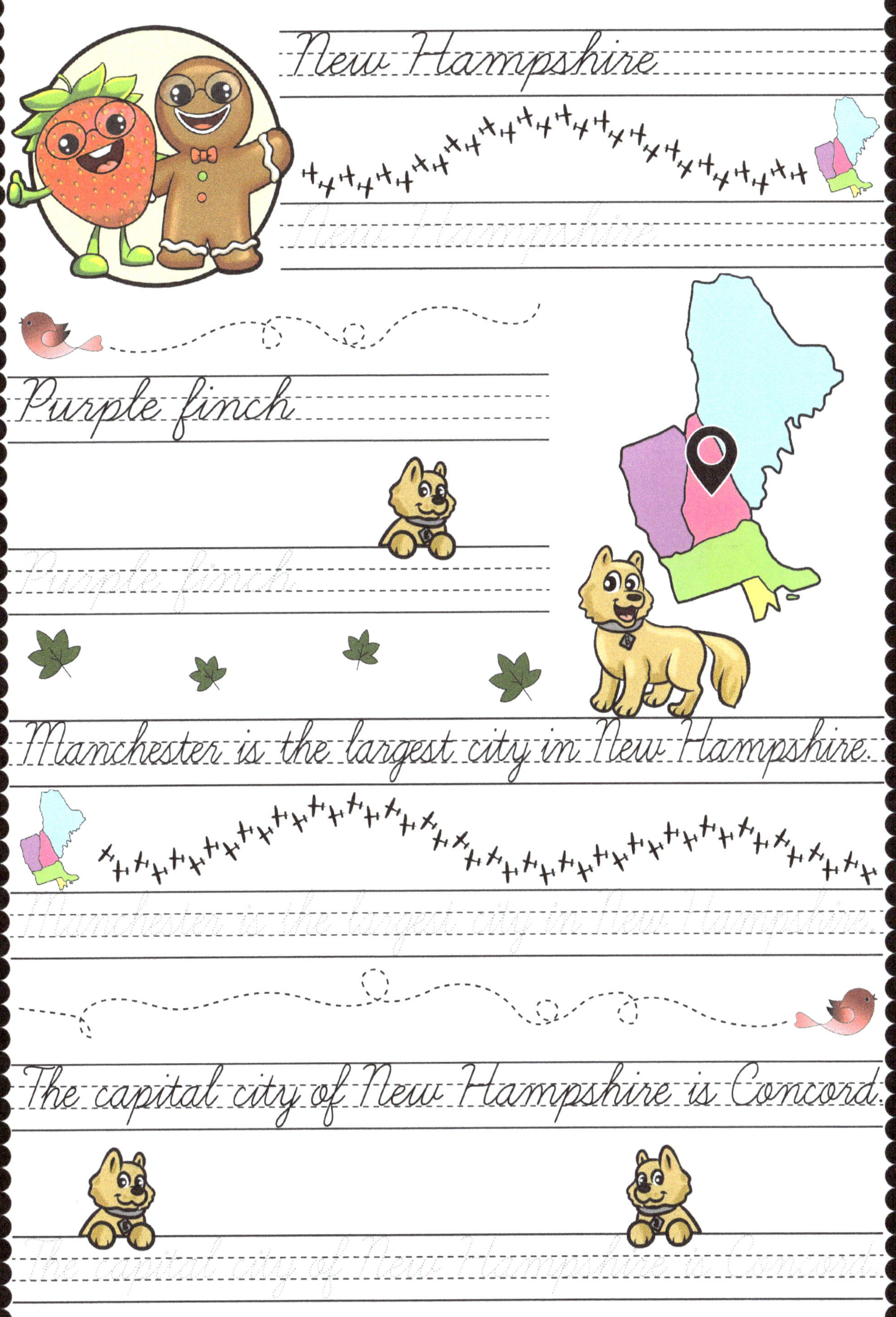

New Hampshire

Purple finch

Manchester is the largest city in New Hampshire.

The capital city of New Hampshire is Concord.

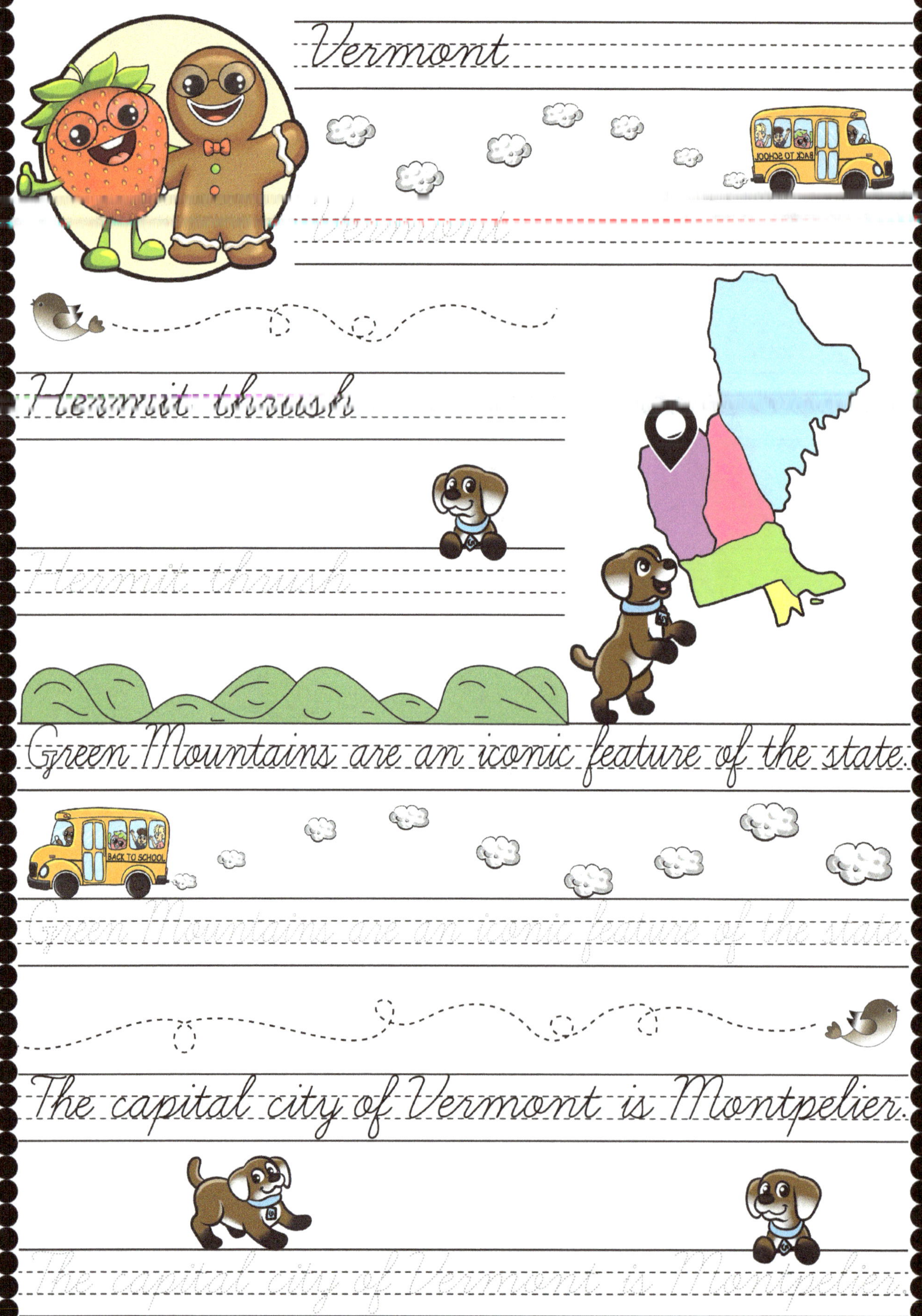

Vermont
Vermont
Hermit thrush
Hermit thrush
Green Mountains are an iconic feature of the state.
Green Mountains are an iconic feature of the state.
The capital city of Vermont is Montpelier.
The capital city of Vermont is Montpelier.

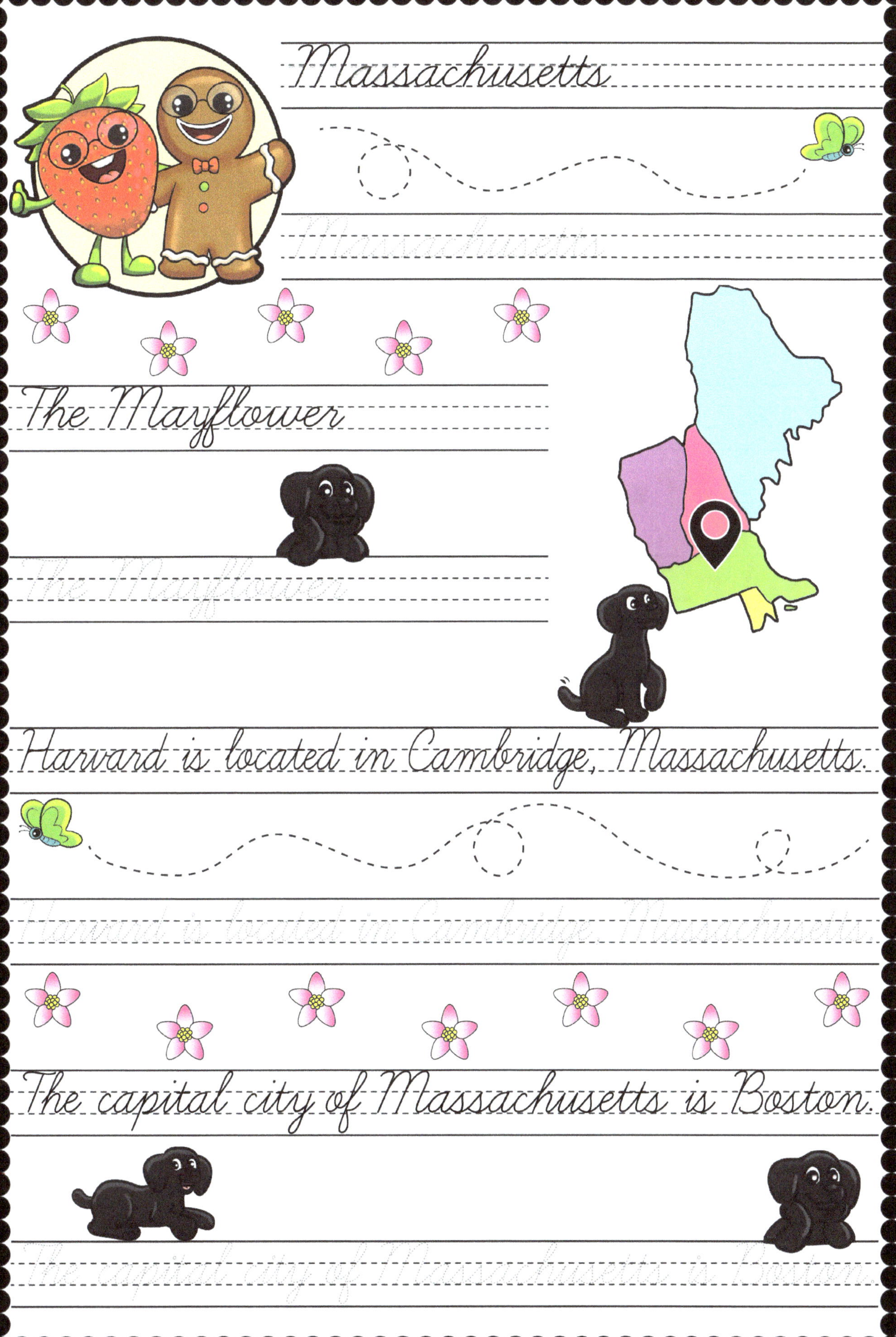

Massachusetts

Massachusetts

The Mayflower

The Mayflower

Harvard is located in Cambridge, Massachusetts.

Harvard is located in Cambridge, Massachusetts.

The capital city of Massachusetts is Boston.

The capital city of Massachusetts is Boston.

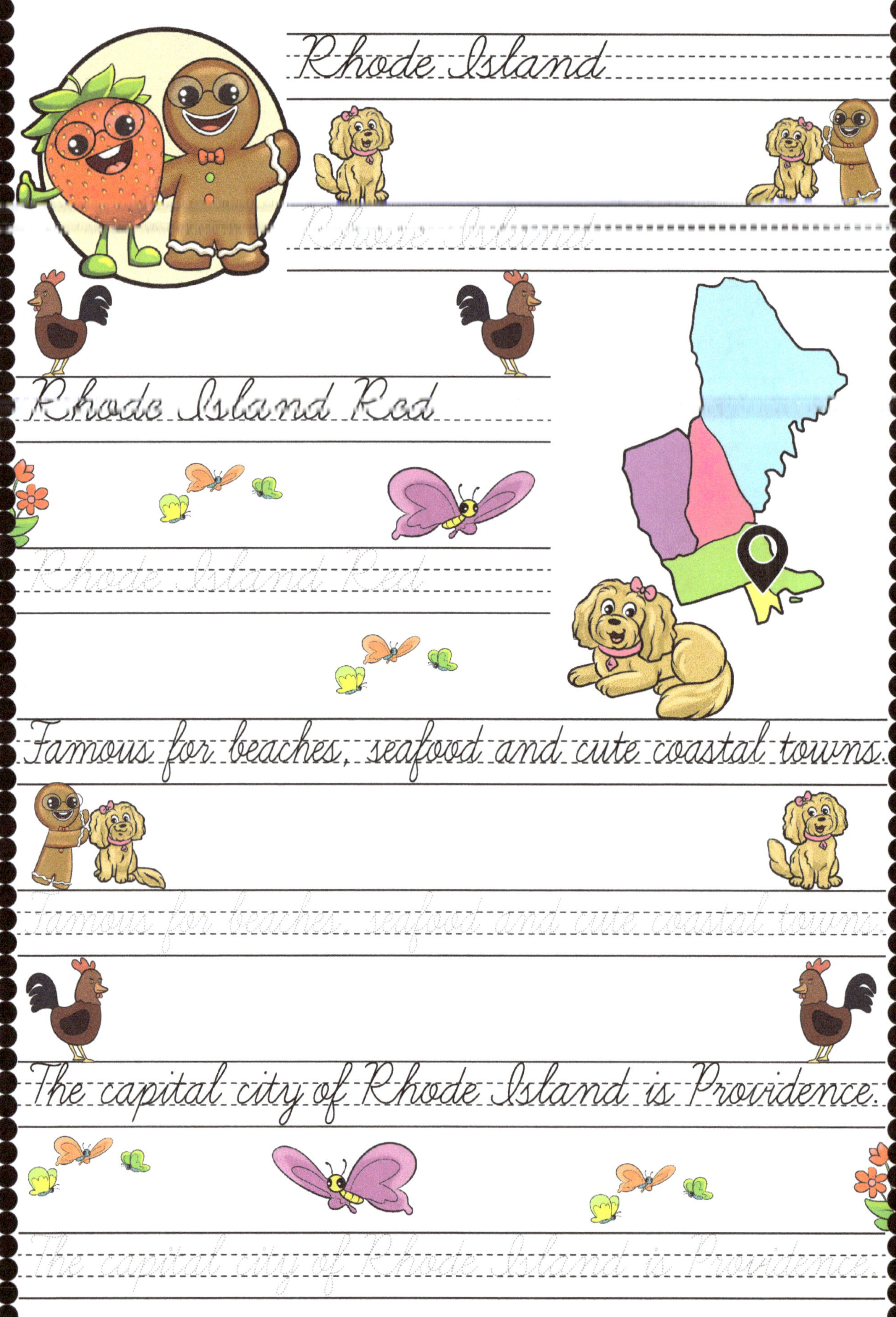

Rhode Island

Rhode Island Red

Famous for beaches, seafood and cute coastal towns.

The capital city of Rhode Island is Providence.

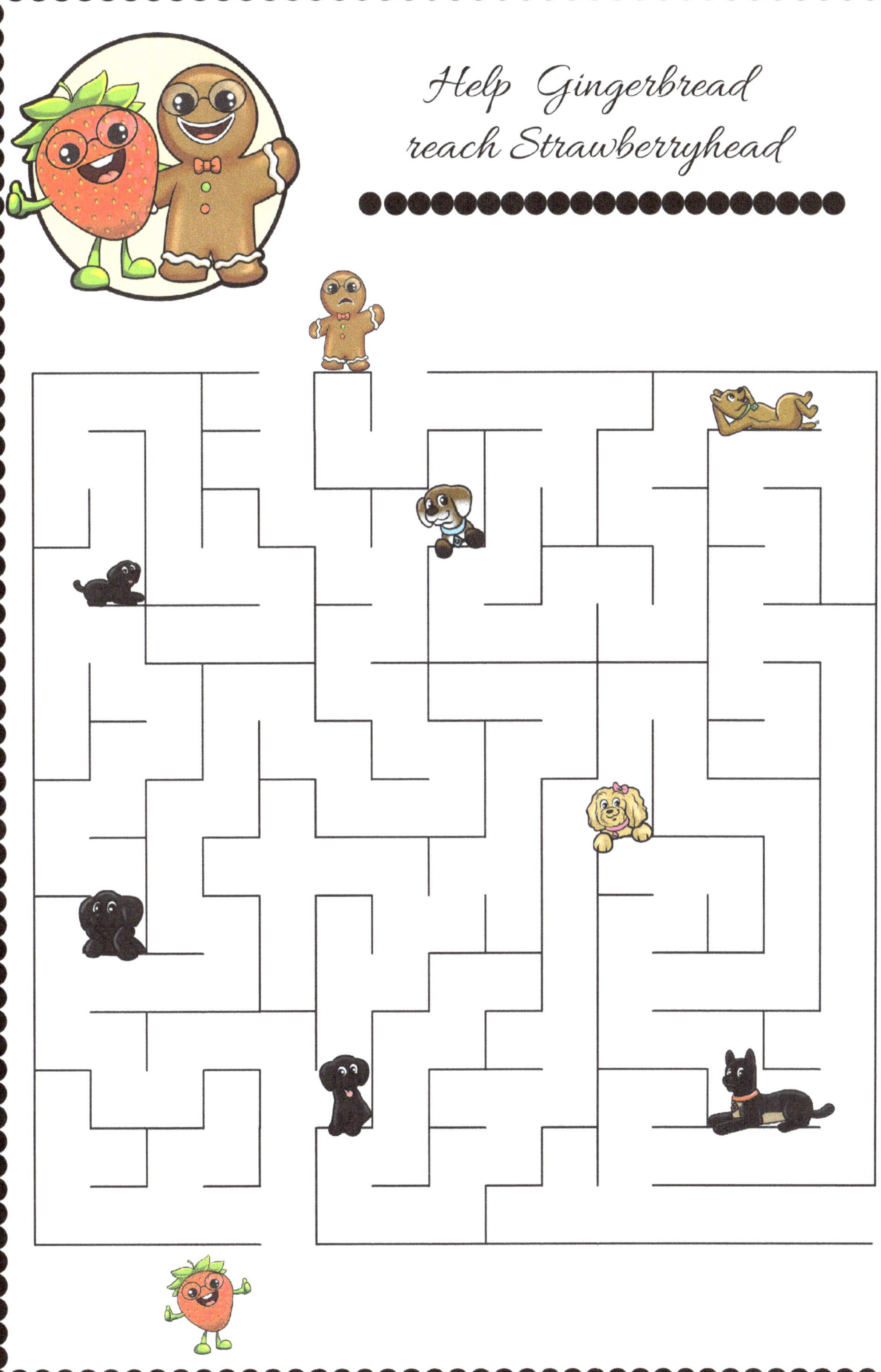

Help Gingerbread
reach Strawberryhead

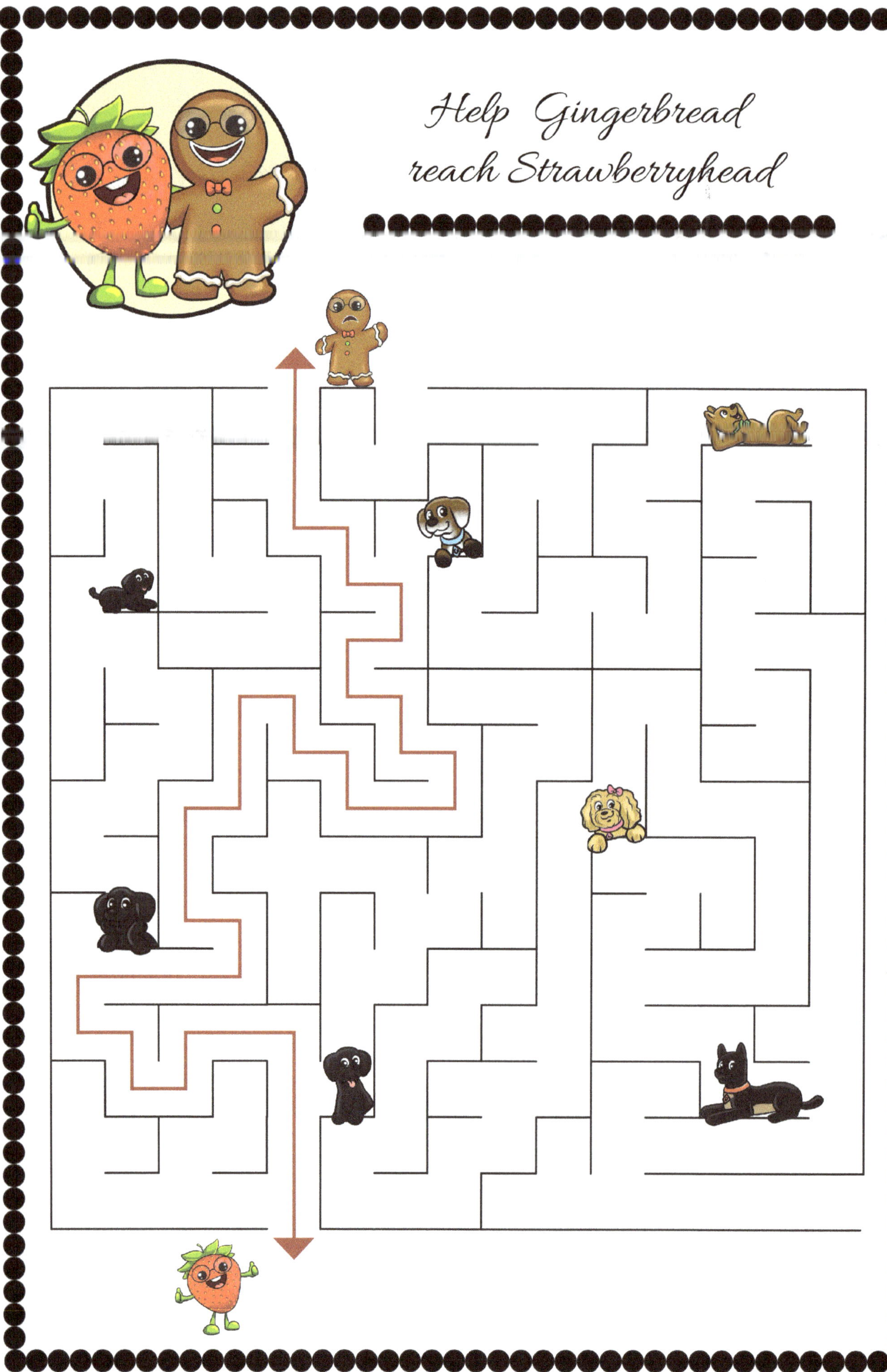

Help Gingerbread
reach Strawberryhead

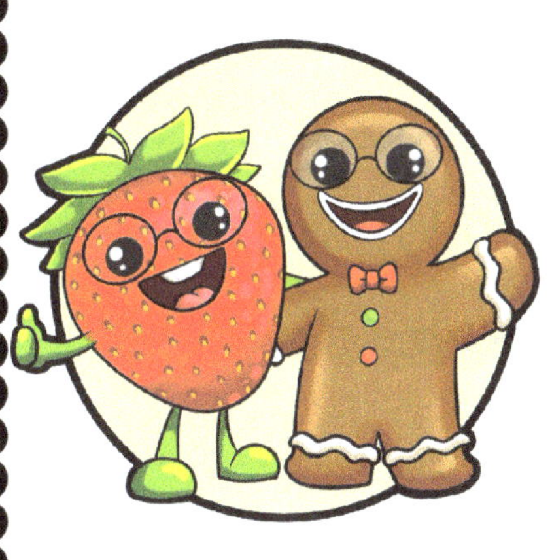

Solve the Problem

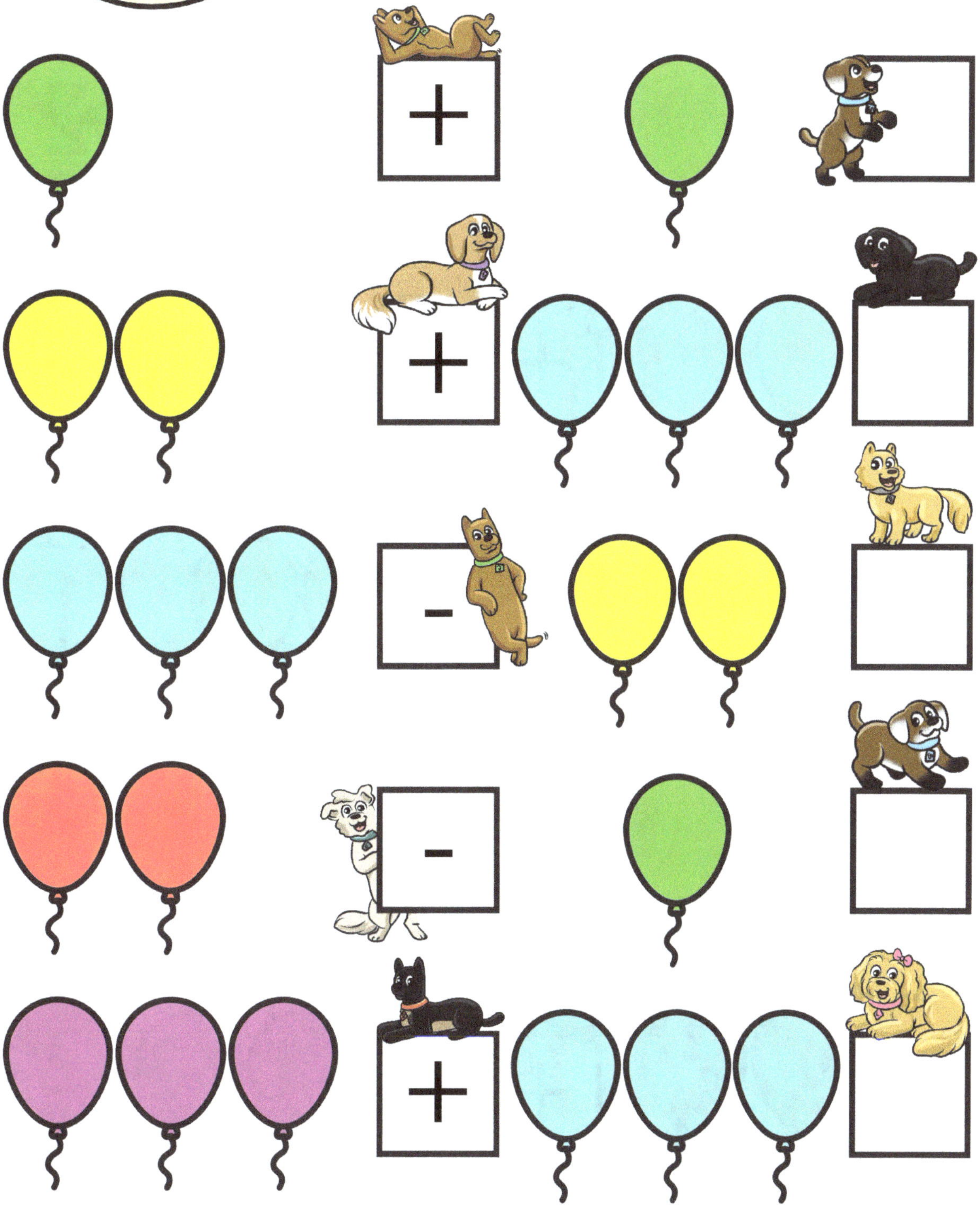

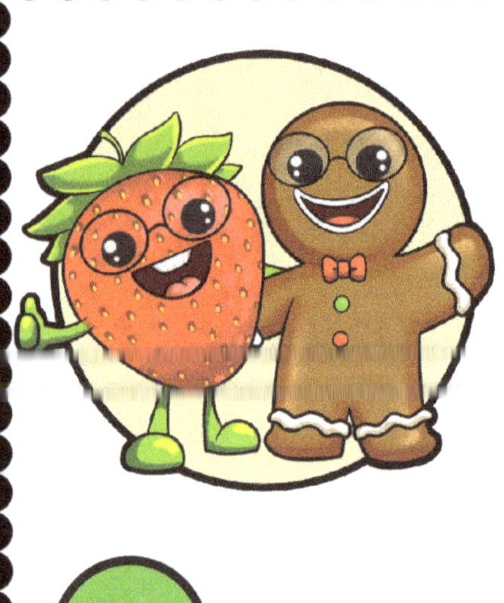

Solve the Problem

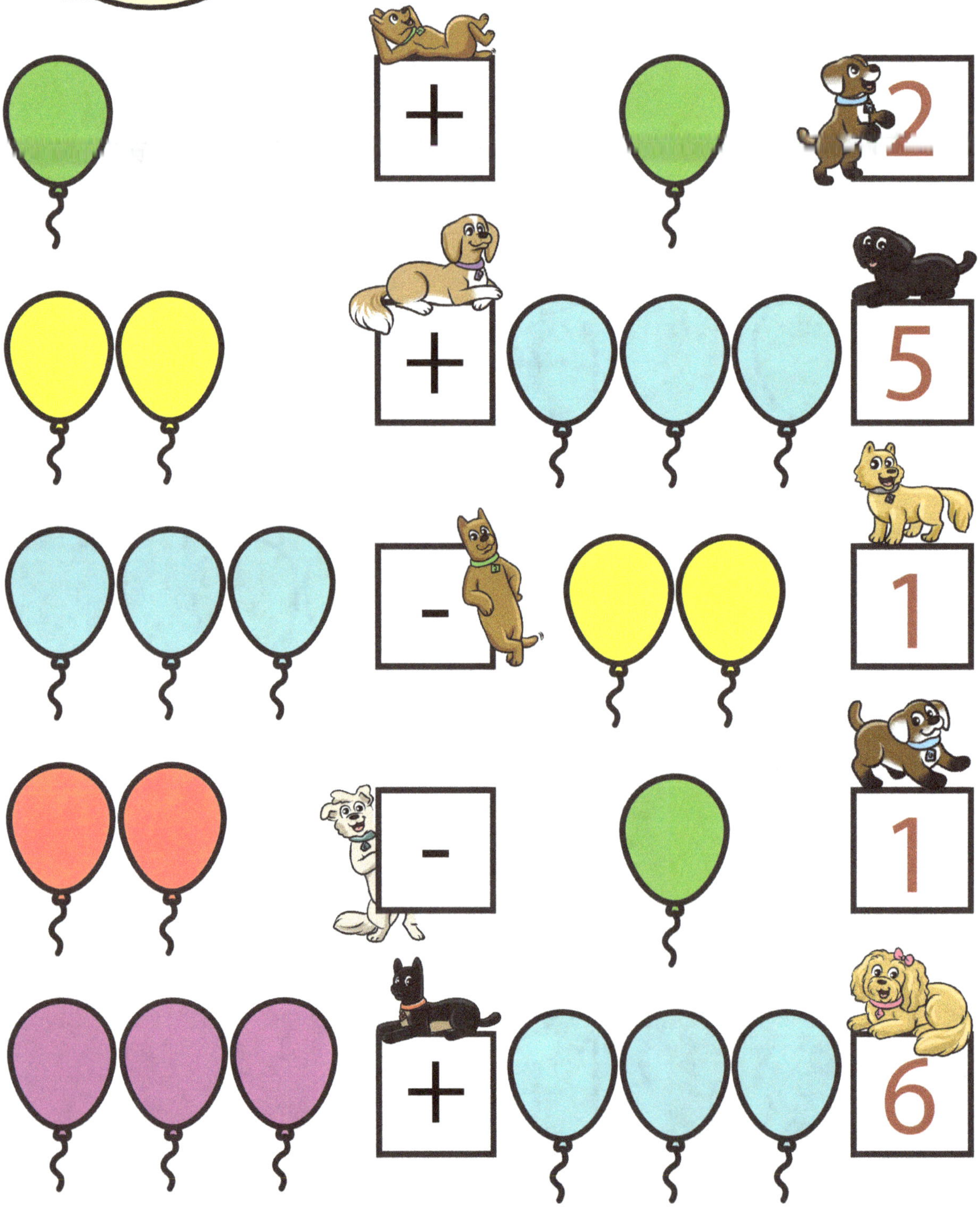

True or False?

The national flag of America has 51 stars.

Evergreen forests are mostly found in hilly regions.

The national game of the USA is Baseball.

The color of the stars on the American flag is white.

The Statue of Liberty is located in Texas.

Parrot is the bird that can mimic human speech.

Kangaroos are the national animal of Ohio.

There are 8 sides in the octagon.

Elephants are the tallest animal in the world.

California is a famous state in the USA.

The national flag of America has 51 stars. 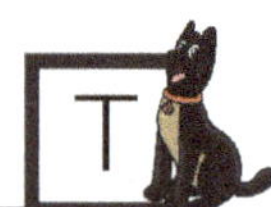 T

Evergreen forests are mostly found in hilly regions. 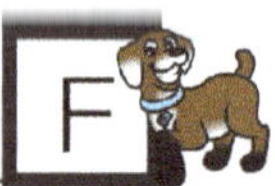 F

The national game of the USA is Baseball. 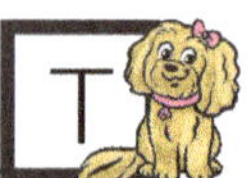 T

The color of the stars on the American flag is white. 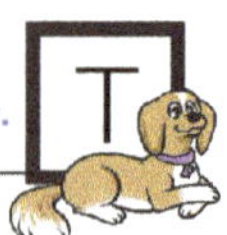 T

The Statue of Liberty is located in Texas. 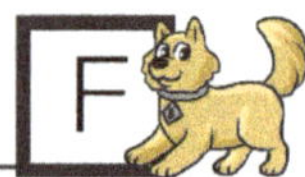 F

Parrot is the bird that can mimic human speech. 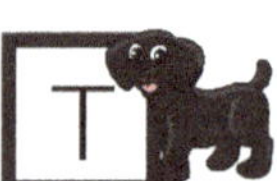 T

Kangaroos are the national animal of Ohio. 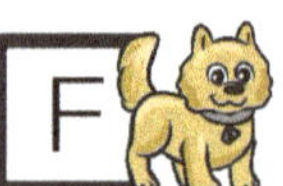 F

There are 8 sides in the octagon. 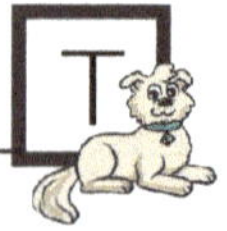 T

Elephants are the tallest animal in the world. 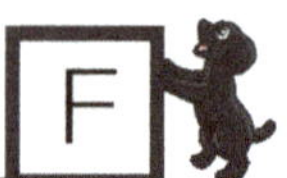 F

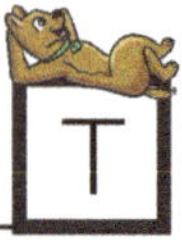

California is a famous state in the USA. T

Color it

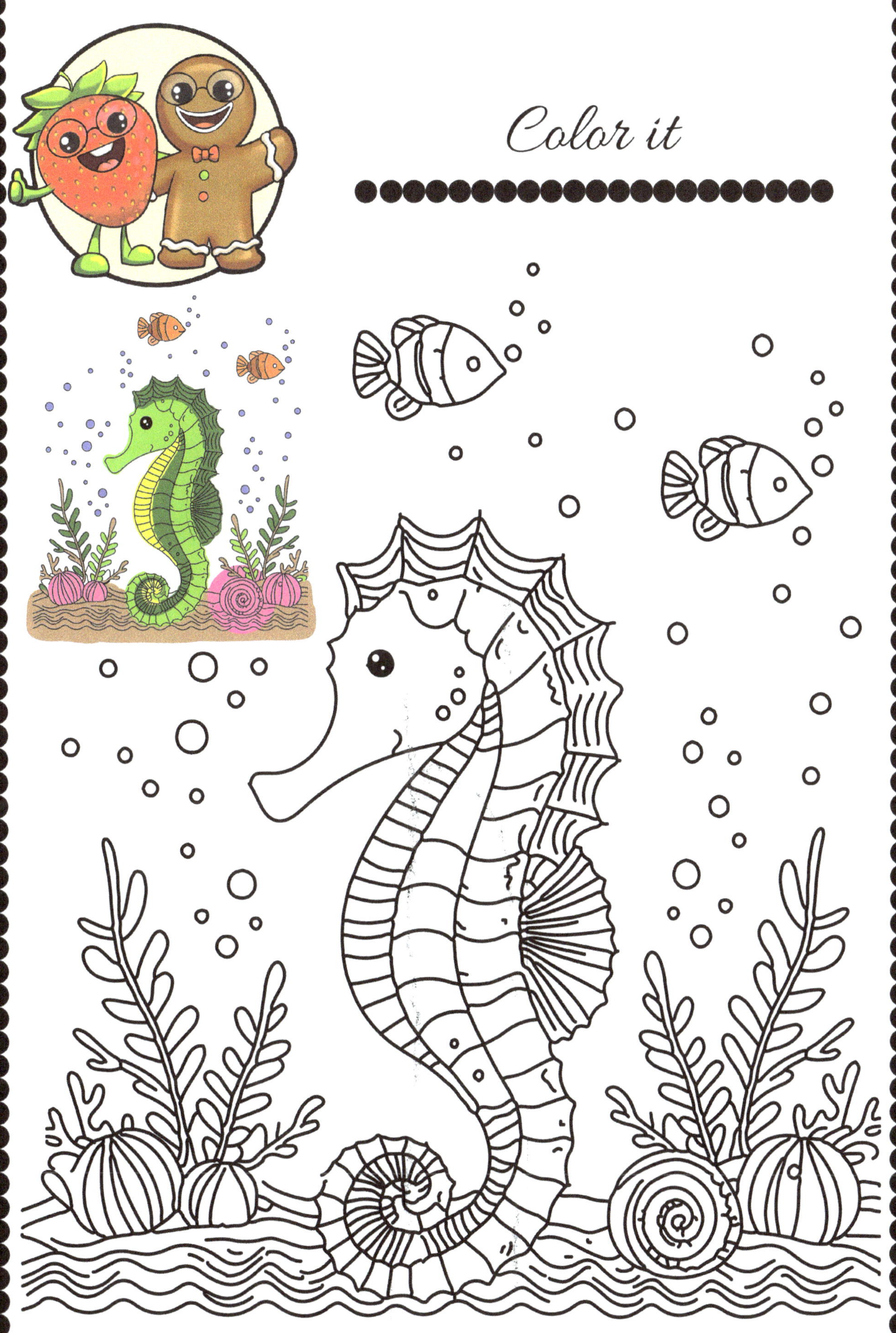

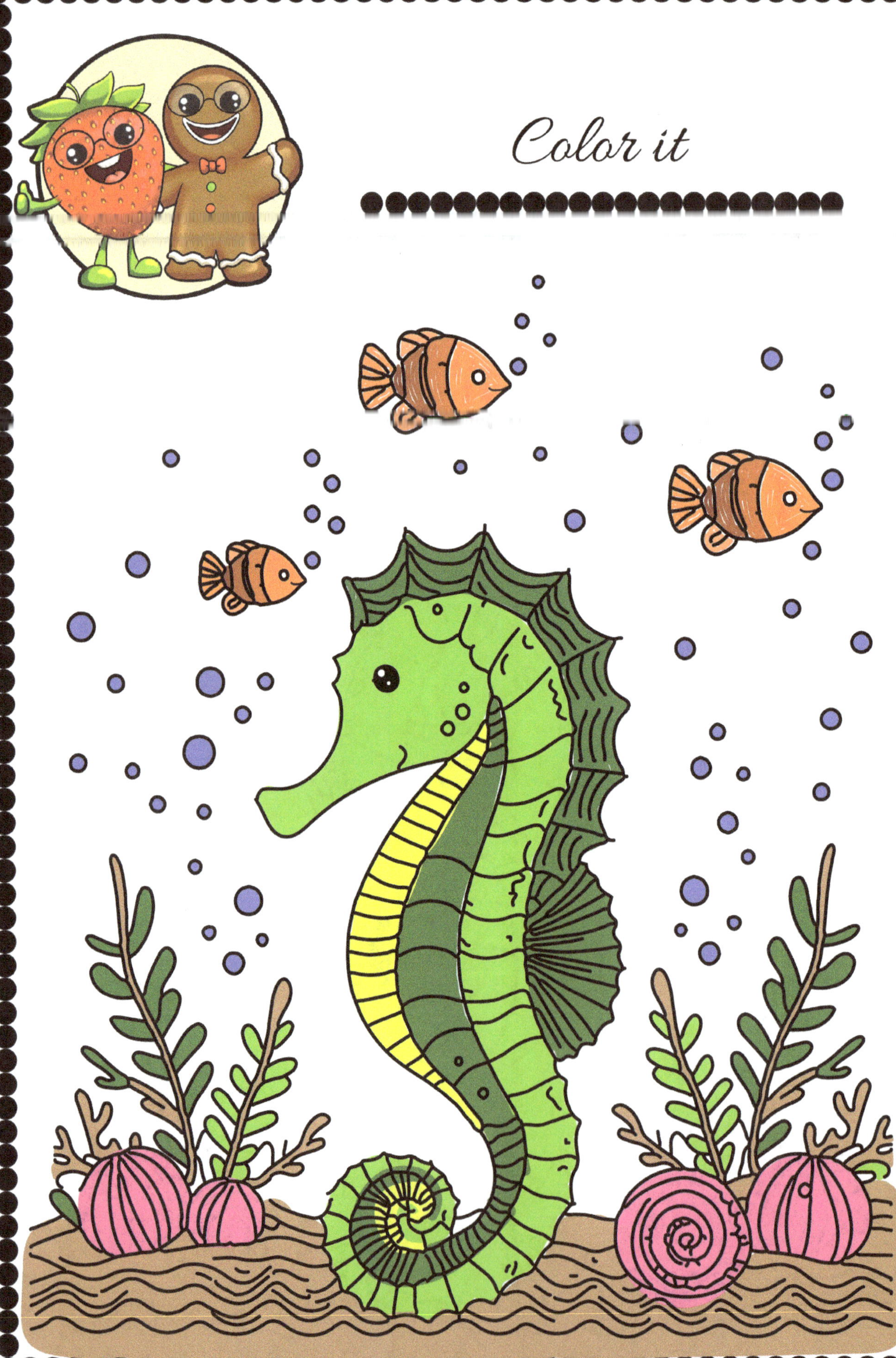
Color it

True or False?

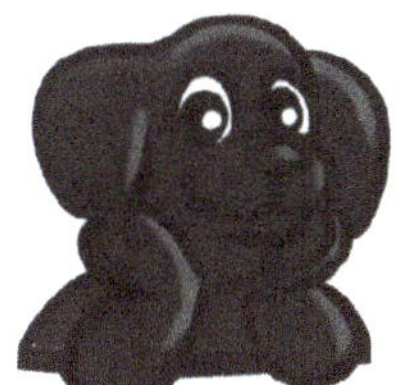

Dogs have a really great sense of smell. ◯

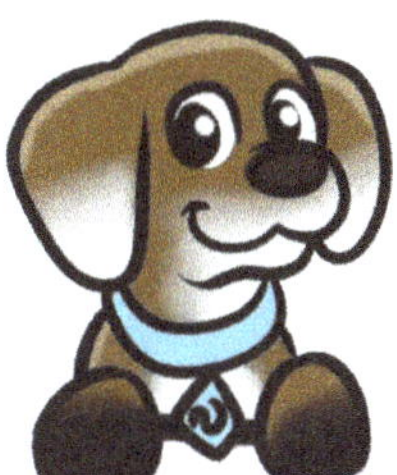

Greyhounds cannot run faster than a cheetah (kind of). ◯

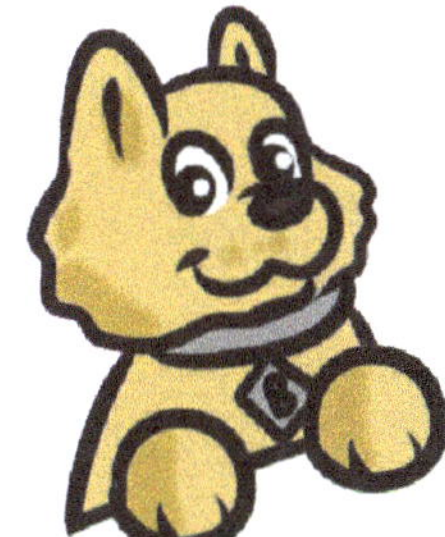

The Great Dane is the tallest dog in the world. ◯

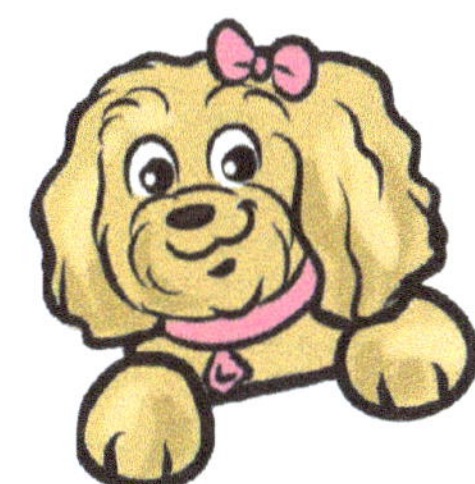

Dogs have two eyelids. ◯

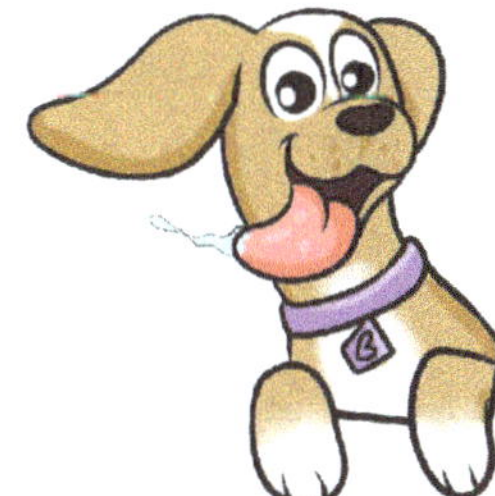

All puppies are born deaf. ◯

True or False?

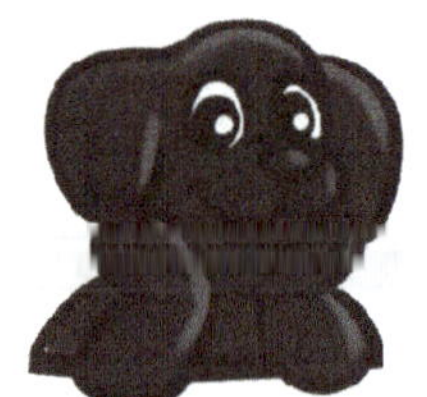
Dogs have a really great sense of smell.
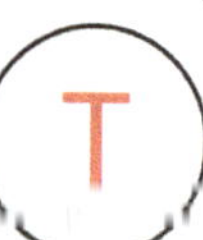 T

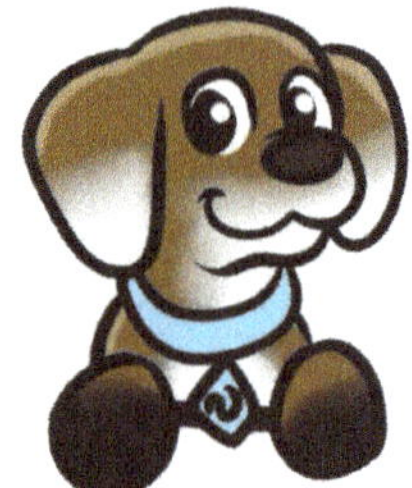
Greyhounds cannot run faster than a cheetah (kind of).
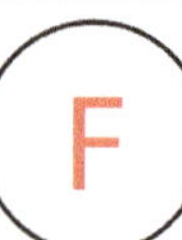 F

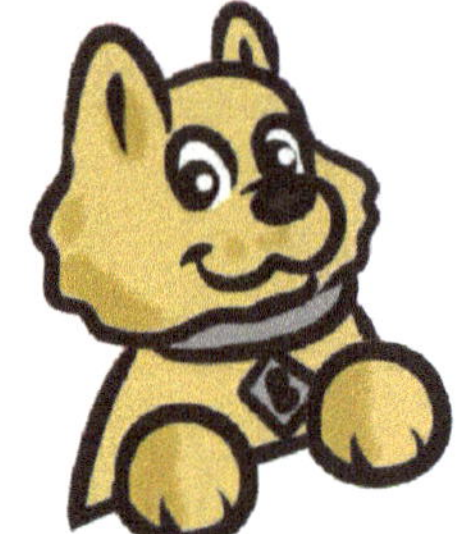
The Great Dane is the tallest dog in the world.
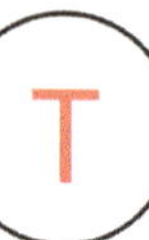 T

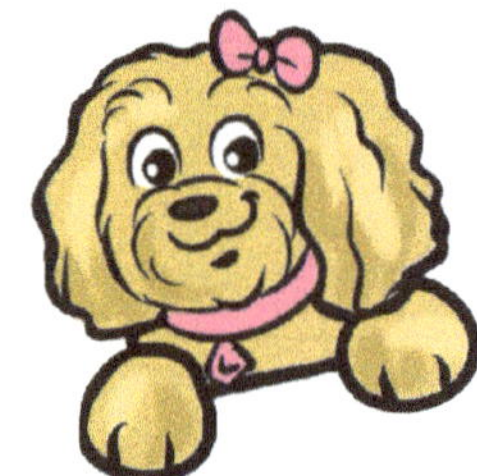
Dogs have two eyelids.
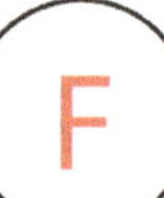 F

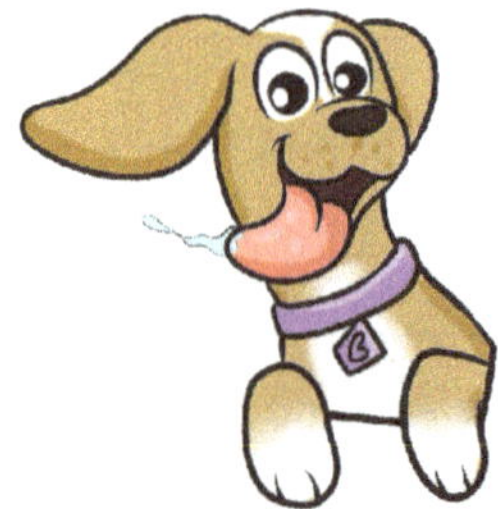
All puppies are born deaf.
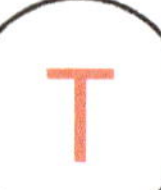 T